Small Group Ministry With Youth

Small Group Ministry With Youth

David R. Veerman

VICTOR BOOKS

A DIVISION OF SCRIPTURE PRESS PUBLICATIONS INC.
USA CANADA ENGLAND

Scripture quotations, unless otherwise indicated, are from the *Holy Bible, New International Version,* © 1973, 1978, 1984, International Bible Society. Used by permission of Zondervan Bible Publishers. Verses marked TLB are taken from *The Living Bible,* © 1971, Tyndale House Publishers, Wheaton, IL 60189. Used by permission.

Copyediting: Laurie Eve Loftin
Cover Design: Joe DeLeon

Library of Congress Cataloging-in-Publication Data

Veerman, David.
   Small group ministry with youth / by David R. Veerman.
     p.   cm.
   Includes bibliographical references.
   ISBN 0-89693-919-7
   1. Church group work with teenagers. 2. Church group work with young adults. I. Title.
   BV4447.V44 1992
   259'.23 – dc20   92-10254
                                                       CIP

---

1 2 3 4 5 6 7 8 9 10 Printing/Year 96 95 94 93 92

DEDICATION

To Mom and Dad, Helen and Marv Veerman. They made our family "small group" of seven a loving and fun place to grow up and learn and grow. And they led us to Christ. I miss you!

CONTENTS

STRICTLY PERSONAL

They kept coming, pushing through the door, stepping over knees, legs, hunched shoulders, and heads bent toward friends in animated conversation. *This is great!* I thought, as the room filled to overflowing with eager high school students, *A youthworker's dream!*

Attendance had been steadily increasing that fall—Campus Life was "in" and the most popular club at the high school. When we reached 100, I was excited. At 150, I was thrilled. And I was overwhelmed when more than 200 came on Monday nights, squeezing into every space in someone's family room, and on warm evenings, standing outside and looking in through the windows or patio doors. Eventually we had to meet in the lounge of an apartment complex.

Why did kids come, disregarding homework pressures, leaving TV and other home comforts, and braving northern weather? For many reasons: because the meetings were fun and exciting, with almost a party atmosphere; because the feeling that "everyone will be there" made it an occasion not to miss; because a solid and dedicated core of upperclassmen who were student leaders brought their friends and helped the meetings run smoothly. But even more important, the real foundation for the ministry was personal relationships. The other staff person and I, along with several volunteers, would spend many hours on campus—during lunch, after school, at school events—being seen, meeting kids, and building relationships. Then at the meetings, I would explain that we would be glad to meet individually with anyone to give counsel and advice, or just to talk things over.

As you might imagine, our ministry plates were full, with personal "appointments" cramming our schedules. Kids were being helped and many were coming to Christ. Campus Life was making an impact on the school, and we were flying high.*

I know this sounds like a wonderful success story, and another frustrating account of "the good old days." But hold on, there's more.

Shortly after we peaked at about 250 at our meetings, the numbers began to slip. A jammed room can be exciting, but it can also be hot, uncomfortable, and noisy. As you might imagine, crowd control was next to impossible. Those who came to learn were frustrated because of the noise. And those who came to have a good time were ticked off because we were always asking them to be quiet. Crowd-breakers became an ordeal, discussions were out of the question, and each wrap-up was a test of wills as I tried to speak between "shhhhhs" and breaks in the chatter. And eventually, of course, the student leaders graduated. Attendance steadily declined, until just two years later, we were lucky if 25 showed up.

In those days, Campus Life (the large, outreach meeting) met every other week, alternating with Insight, geared for Christians. The purpose of the Insight meetings was to help kids grow in their faith. Centered around relevant topics, each meeting would feature lively discussion and Bible study. Attendance at Insight grew along with Campus Life; eventually, anywhere between 60 and 90 kids would come on alternate Monday evenings. But as our numbers increased and the rooms became crowded and noisy, our effectiveness dropped, and the format evolved into semi-weekly lectures. Eventually Insight attendance also fell dramatically.

Looking back on those roller-coaster years, I can see the problem—we weren't prepared for success. The school was our mission field, so our target numbered 2500. But when we began to "reach" a substantial number of those students, we weren't prepared for the next step. Certainly our philosophy of ministry was biblical and sound, emphasizing relationships and person-centeredness (and we were doing the right things in our personal ministry). But despite all our contacting and appointments, Campus Life had become program-centered and meeting-oriented. And when the meetings became ineffective, the ministry suffered.

Another problem was that we were advertising what we couldn't deliver, promising friendship and personal attention. Think about it—how could a handful of staff evangelize, disciple, and meet the needs of all those young people? (And my territory involved TWO high schools, so double that amount.) Yet kids we met on campus came to see us (and then we forgot their names); kids we had friendships with wanted to be with us (but we were too busy meeting others); kids who needed help wanted counsel (but practically had to stand in line for appointments); kids who responded to the Gospel needed to grow in their faith (but we had no time to spend with them). In a sense, the personal ministry had become reduced to "maintenance," and campus visits to "marketing."

What could we have done to deal with these problems? At the risk of oversimplification, let me suggest that the answer lies in two words—SMALL GROUPS. If we had established a network of small groups, we would have been able to maintain personal attention, provide opportunities for growth, and respond to special needs in the group. I know that what I have just said is easier said than done, but I am convinced that it's worth the effort—because it can work.

Before I go any further, let me explain that by "small group," I mean *a group of 4–10 young people and a leader who meet together regularly and are committed to each other, to the group, and to learning and growing together.* That's the basic definition we will use in this book.

Ted, another young man on our YFC staff, took a different approach to reaching his schools. Instead of trying to minister to the entire student body by himself through one-on-one contacts and large meetings, Ted recruited and mobilized a team of volunteers. Together they made campus visits and built a relational foundation. Then, as more and more kids became involved, Ted assigned each volunteer to 5–10 kids who came regularly to Campus Life or who needed special attention. The volunteer's task was to focus his or her efforts on this handful of kids and, if possible, develop a small group with them.

Training and caring for volunteers takes time, so Ted didn't go on campus himself as much as I did—and his attendance never grew into immense proportions. But his Campus Life meetings averaged a solid 100, without the wide fluctuations that I experienced. Through the small group approach, Ted was able to minister to hundreds of students each year.

Of course many youth workers don't have the problem of too many kids in the program. In fact, they may have the opposite problem—too few. But large attendance is not the only reason for taking this ministry approach. Through small groups, you can train, teach, counsel, disciple, and even evangelize. Through small groups, you can dig deeper into the Word. Through small groups, you can multiply the personal, relational side of the ministry.†

Over the years, I've seen a lot of youth ministry. I am convinced that working through small groups can be a responsible and effective strategy for reaching young people for Christ.

That's what this book is about—ministering to young people through small groups. In the first half, we'll discuss topics such as:

- getting started—how to get kids involved, get organized, and get going
- group dynamics—how to analyze the personal chemistry and interaction in a group and use it to your advantage in the ministry
- leadership—how to lead a group and keep it on track toward the stated purpose and objectives
- discussion—how to facilitate discussion and keep it focused

In the second half of the book, we'll analyze several case studies of small group ministry—real-life examples of men and women who are making it work. Let's get going!

*During the school year, the administration of this school surveyed students concerning their activities and interests. In a student body of 2500, 1500 said they were "active" in Campus Life.

†Warning: just because your group is small, don't assume that you automatically have a "small group." Size is just one of the factors in an effective small group ministry.

ONE
WISE WHYS
Learning the Rationale for Small Group Ministry with Young People

hat's missing from this sentence?

"One da   in Ma , Harr   asked Sall   to Gar 's part .
Sall   was so happ   that all she could sa   was ' es, es,
es!' Then she and Mar   went to bu   a dress."

The obvious answer is "the Ys." "So what?" you ask. Well, that sentence illustrates how people sometimes jump into ministry. Without the "whys," the ministry will be incomplete at best, making very little sense, and may even head in the wrong direction. So before we dive into the "hows," let's take a closer look at the "whys," the rationale for small groups. In other words, why should we bother with this approach? Isn't it enough to sponsor exciting events, exotic trips, exhilarating speakers, and excellent meetings? No, it's not. As great as all those ministry tools are, without love they are worth nothing (see 1 Corinthians 13:1-3). And one way to minister with love is through small groups.

Kids aren't customers, statistics, or bodies—they are special, individual people, each created by God in His image (see Genesis 1:27). That's why any truly responsible and biblical youth ministry must be caring, loving, and personal. And today, kids need the personal touch more than ever.

In a small group, members can receive individual attention from the leader and can build close relationships with other group members. Also, education and communication can be enhanced in this setting. That's why pastors, chaplains, counselors, and others have found small groups to be effective with people of all ages. But small group ministry is especially needed for young people because of the following factors.

KIDS FEEL LOST

Imagine the frenzied excitement at a rock concert, a state championship basketball game, or a giant New Year's Eve party. It's fun to be part of the crowd, and kids love it. But they can also be lost in that same crowd, pushed and pulled by group pressures, their identity engulfed and merged.

A friend and I drove to downtown New Orleans early on Tuesday morning. We wanted to be in the front row to watch the Krewes of Zulu and Rex, and so we staked our claim at the curb on Canal Street. But as the Mardi Gras crowd grew, we found ourselves in a sea of bodies, filling the street. When the parades came, the sea would part for every float, pushing us back, far away from the action. It was fun, reaching for "throws" and yelling at costumed riders, but it was also frightening, being carried against our will by the crowd.

ADOLESCENTS AND PEERS

During early adolescence the most significant movement is from parents and family to peers as the reference group. This movement is of vital importance because the young person begins looking primarily toward peers for feeling accepted, for confirmation of personal 'okayness' and for agreement concerning values, beliefs, ideas, and feelings.

From *Counseling Teenagers* by Dr. Keith Olson (Group Books, 1984), page 32.

For young people today, their crowd of peers means everything. Wanting desperately to be accepted and liked, they will do almost anything to belong. When kids are "in," it's exciting to be where the action is. But being part of the crowd can also be frightening for kids, especially when they feel pushed in the wrong direction against their will.

Students may also feel lost in the crowd simply by the sheer number of people involved. In a school of 2000 and a class of 500, who cares about that lowly freshman guy, the shy junior, or anyone out of the limelight? At least that's what those kids often think. And it's a fact that students at both ends of the spectrum (the "stars" or the trouble-makers) seem to get all the attention, with those in the middle forgotten or ignored by teachers, counselors, youth sponsors, student leaders, and even parents. Since the vast majority of young people fall somewhere in the middle, it's safe to say that most kids feel insignificant and lost.

Kids need a place to be known and appreciated for who they are. They need a place to belong and to be accepted. A small group can be that place.

KIDS ARE LONELY

The pervasive malaise of our time and culture is loneliness. In this impersonal world, people feel isolated, cut off. The technological explosion has heightened the problem, with people communicating through electric impulses, microchips, and dots on paper. Computers, modems, facsimile transmitters, cellular phones, and other hi-tech appliances pull the world closer electronically but push us apart personally.

As the bombs and missles began to rain on Baghdad, the world watched and listened in stunned silence. Millions of Americans sat in front of their televisions and heard the latest word on the war, transmitted by satellite as the events unfolded. Sitting alone in our rooms, we were close to the world, yet isolated from each other. Who knows what emotions and thoughts filled millions of hearts and minds? We live in the age of information in which everyone seems to know everything, but nobody knows who we are.

"Norm!" A welcome chorus greets the heavyset figure wrapped in a rumpled overcoat as he enters and walks to his place at the bar. He is at home, with friends who know and accept him. As viewers watch their TV sets, they identify with Norm and the other characters and their need for friendship—and "Cheers" becomes a hit. The theme song says: "Sometimes you want to go where everybody knows your name...." We want to be known—we don't want to be lonely.

Kids are not immune to these feelings of isolation, especially with the rise of divorce, single-parent homes, two-income families, latch-key children, and so forth. Often a young person will leave from and return to an empty house each school day.

LONELINESS

Loneliness is the painful awareness that we lack meaningful contact with others. It involves a feeling of inner emptiness which can be accompanied by sadness, discouragement, a sense of isolation, restlessness, anxiety, and an intense desire to be wanted and needed by someone. Lonely people often feel "left out," unwanted, or rejected, even when they are surrounded by others.

From *Christian Counseling* by Dr. Gary Collins (Word Publishing, 1980), page 72.

Kids are lonely, and they need relationships. That's why friends are so important to them; it's why they form cliques; and it's why they spend hours on the phone.

Human beings were not meant "to live alone" (see Genesis 2:18). We were created as relational beings. We need love, friendship, understanding, care, touch—relationships. No wonder we keep looking for love.

A small group can meet that need; it can be the place

where an isolated young person connects with someone else. In an impersonal world, a small group can be the place where everyone knows your name.

KIDS ARE AFRAID

"Ready or not, here I come!" Dad opens his eyes and slowly walks through the rooms of the house, pretending to look for his little girl, and ignoring her giggles as she "hides" in the closet. Playing hide-and-seek can be fun for young children. But for older kids it's not a game, as they hide their real opinions, ideas, dreams, and emotions. Often behind a smiling facade lie unspoken fears and unsettling feelings. And what they hide is not always negative; goals, aspirations, thoughts, and questions are also beneath the surface.

AFRAID
Why am I afraid to tell you who I am? I'm afraid to tell you who I am because you may not like who I am, and that's all I have.

Father John Powell, S.J.

Why do they hide inside? They're afraid of ridicule and looking stupid. Remember, these kids have probably been mocked for their awkward attempts at socialization, especially with the opposite sex. They may have been blasted and even punished by parents for speaking their minds. They could have been humiliated by coaches for making suggestions or talking back. Perhaps they have been hurt by boyfriends or girlfriends for expressing their feelings. They could have been embarrassed by friends who broke confidences and passed along secrets. And they may have been penalized by teachers for asking tough questions.

It's easier and safer to hide.

Can you imagine someone admitting a drug problem in a

large meeting, or expressing serious doubts about God at church? Or how about someone asking what seems to be a simple question about life, or telling the youth group that he or she has thought about suicide?

But how can people find answers if they don't ask questions? How can they find direction if they don't admit they're lost? How can they find solutions if they don't face up to their problems? How can they find help if they don't share their needs?

Kids need a place to talk, a safe place where they can say whatever is on their minds without fear of ridicule or retaliation. They need a place where they can ask any question and find answers, express any feeling and find acceptance, and share any secret and find trust.

A small group can be that safe place. Secure in commitment to each other and to the group, kids can stop hiding and be themselves.

KIDS ARE LEARNING

Adolescence is a time of rapid growth in all areas. Young people are learning vast amounts about themselves and the world. Generally speaking, our schools do an excellent job educating young minds—teaching them algebra, biology, geography, social studies, English, history, foreign languages, and a variety of other subjects. But our schools do very little to deal with the most basic and vital issues: the meaning of life, the existence of God, life after death, values, morals, and spiritual truths.

That's why we're in the ministry—to share with kids the truth of God's Word, the Good News about Christ, and the life-changing power of the Holy Spirit.

While effective communication can take place in a large group setting or one-on-one, the small group experience provides some exceptional advantages. Each small group participant can receive:
- *information* and *insight* from others in the group;
- *acceptance* and *encouragement* from people who care;
- *time* to get into issues in depth;

- *accountability* for commitments made;
- *reinforcement* for positive ideas, thoughts, and decisions;
- *support* when struggling with difficulties or problems;
- a strong feeling of *camaradarie,* knowing that everyone is learning and growing together.

PROVIDING A CONTEXT

"Close relationships among the members of God's family provide a context for applying biblical truth, promote unity and caring among the members, meet spiritual and emotional needs, furnish a setting for lifestyle evangelism, and in short, demonstrate the Body of Christ in action.

"I am convinced that small groups provide the ideal format to accomplish these requirements."

From "What's the Big Deal about Small Groups?" by Neal McBride, *Discipleship Journal,* September/ October, 1990.

Jesus taught a small group of disciples. In addition to instructing these men (e.g. Luke 8:9-15), Jesus worked through problems with them (e.g. Luke 8:22-25), allowed them to watch Him minister (e.g. Luke 8:40-56), gave them assignments (e.g. Luke 9:1-6), affirmed them (e.g. Matthew 16:13-20), corrected them (e.g. Matthew 16:21-23), and encouraged them (e.g. John 16:31-33). Christ's small group changed the world.

A small group can be a great place to learn.

Small groups are needed because kids are LOST in the crowd, LONELY in an impersonal world, AFRAID to admit problems and reveal their true selves, and LEARNING to live. Having said all that, however, I must add a disclaimer— small groups per se will not guarantee successful ministry; they're not magic. Effective ministry is determined by a number of factors, including the needs and personalities of the kids, the environment, the skill of the minister, and, most important of all, the work of the Holy Spirit. But a small group can be an excellent way to provide the atmosphere for genuine ministry to occur.

Well, I've preached enough. If I've been effective, you should be chomping at the bit to get going. So let's get into the practical side. What's next? What's the first step? Check out the next chapter and find out.

TWO
STIR CRAZY
Gathering the Ingredients for Effective Small Groups

1 3/4 C. flour

1 tsp. baking soda

1/2 tsp. salt

1/2 C. sugar

1/2 C. firmly packed brown sugar

1/2 C. margarine

1/2 C. peanut butter

1 egg

2 TBSP. milk

1 tsp. vanilla extract

Combine all ingredients in large mixing bowl. Mix on low speed until dough forms. Shape dough into small balls; roll in sugar; place on ungreased cookie sheet. . . .

T hat's a cookie recipe. If you collect the ingredients, stir them thoroughly, and follow the rest of the directions, you'll have three dozen tasty morsels. Success is assured.

Wouldn't it be great if youth ministry could be that way—if all we had to do was to follow the directions, step by step? The recipe for a successful small group might read:

---

1 sr. boy—medium height, musical, bright

1 sr. boy—athletic, warm, enthusiastic

1 sr. girl—motivated, sincere, happy

1 sr. girl—short, generous, knowledgeable

2 jr. boys—friendly, thoughtful, coordinated

1 jr. girl—outgoing, attractive, humorous

1 jr. girl—sensitive, caring, spiritual

1 adult leader—charismatic, loving, witty, intelligent, skilled, articulate

Combine all ingredients in comfortable family room. Mix together for one hour a week for six weeks. Shape into disciples.

Obviously, that won't work (although it sure looks good on paper)—there are too many variables, too many human factors. Unfortunately, however, that's what a lot of ministry plans sound like—recipes—just add kids and stir.

I've seen small group ministry strategies with that approach. "It's easy," the spokesman says as he distributes photocopied ministry plans. "Organize everyone into groups of eight and assign a leader to each group. Then have them meet once a week for eight weeks (for an hour each time) to go over the lessons."

But it's NOT easy. In fact, it can seem next to impossible when the kids don't want to be organized, especially if they're not in the same group as their friends (and then all they want to do is talk and mess around).

My warning is simple: beware of paper plans that are idealized and removed from reality. Before jumping into ANY ministry strategy, picture it with REAL people, the kids and staff in your situation. So before you design a small group ministry, you should answer these questions:

- What's our purpose? (What do we hope to accomplish?)
- Where will the kids come from?
- Why will the kids agree to meet in small groups?
- Who will lead these groups?
- What will we do after we get organized?

Helping you answer these questions is what this chapter is all about. The questions are early in the book, because without the right answers, the ministry strategy will fail.

PURPOSE, PHILOSPHY, PLAN

The first step for any project is to look at it from the broad perspective, to think it through and count the cost before you get started. This begins with deciding on the *purpose* ("Why are we doing this? What do we hope to accomplish? If this is successful, what will be the result?").

Small groups can be used to accomplish a variety of objectives, many of which I've stated or implied in the previous chapter. And the last half of this book will profile several small group ministries that have been designed to meet a number of different needs. Here are some possible purposes for small groups:

- personal ministry (breaking down a large group to give kids the personal touch)
- leadership development (training kids to take leadership in the church)

- spiritual growth (helping kids mature in their faith)
- Bible study (getting kids into the Word)
- follow-up (teaching new Christians the basics of the faith)
- support (helping those with special needs; for example: children of divorce, kids with alcoholic parents, etc.)
- evangelism (reaching non-Christian young people through discussion groups)
- training (teaching Christian kids how to reach their friends for Christ)
- community-building (helping youth experience the Body of Christ in action)

Of course it is possible to combine a couple of these purposes (for example, you could help kids grow in the faith through Bible study, or you could build community while doing leadership training, etc.). And your purpose may be different than any of those stated above. Regardless of the direction you take, the point is that you should articulate a purpose for your ministry in general—and specifically—for this ministry approach. Don't jump into small groups because you bought this book or because other youth ministers have been effective. Answer the WHY question: Why are you doing this? What do you hope to accomplish?

Next, we come to *philosophy*. This refers to the ministry non-negotiables, the philosophical grid by which all ministry is evaluated. Your philosophy determines the parameters of your methods, describing HOW the ministry must be carried out. You may, for example, believe that every teaching aspect of your ministry must be tied to Scripture. One of your non-negotiables may be that the ministry must be relational. Or you may have strong feelings about how much time kids should be asked to give to your program; the time the leaders should spend with kids individually, outside of the group; the qualifications of group leaders; or the curriculum used. (Your church may have much to say about the philosophy.)

Think through your philosophy and write it down. Your purpose and philosophy will then shape your ministry *plan*. The plan is simply WHAT you will do, consistent with your philosophy, to accomplish your purpose. This is the nuts and bolts of the ministry, or, to use our recipe analogy, the "ingredients," the "kitchen," and the schedule.

Here's how the purpose, philosophy, and plan might look for a church youth group where several kids had just become Christians after an outreach event.

Purpose: To help new Christians grow in their faith by teaching them the basics of the Christian life.

Philosophy: This program must build the youth group (and existing youth programs), not detract from it; it must be short-term; it must focus on the Bible, with emphasis on application.

Plan: Janet will talk to the kids individually (all ten) and invite them to meet with her to organize the small group. At that meeting, Janet will explain the purpose of the group, how long each meeting will last, and how many weeks they will meet (six weeks). Group members will decide on the best time and place for them to meet each week and will commit to being at every meeting. Janet will use YFC's "First Steps" and "Guaranteed in Writing" as the curriculum.

After thinking through your purpose, philosophy, and plan, the next step is to consider who will be in the mix, the people who will make the recipe work.

INGREDIENTS

Youth

This is the most important ingredient for any aspect of youth ministry, the youths themselves. But often we take them for granted, assuming that kids will get involved in whatever we suggest. Reality would suggest otherwise. I can think of many examples of ministry plans that looked great on paper, but fell apart because nobody came.

Several years ago when I was in Youth for Christ, someone from the national office wrote a small group strategy for reaching neighborhoods and high school campuses. The idea was to get kids into groups of 7–10 and, eventually, by multiplying these groups, hundreds would be involved. The math was impeccable, but the proposal failed to answer the most basic questions: Where would the kids come from? And who would get them there? It assumed that a staff person could go into a community or onto a campus and find a pool of kids who were eager for the chance to be involved.

Don't assume that small groups or any other ministry program will work automatically and easily. Nothing can substitute for the basics and the hard work of the ministry: spending time with kids and building relationships. You have to have a foundation before you can build on it. Before you divide into small groups, you have to have a group of kids to divide.

COMMITMENT

The small group should gain a commitment from the guys or girls to be a part of the group. If a person feels forced into a small group, then he will most likely come late, skip meetings, or say at a later date, "I didn't want to be a part of this group anyway." If it's his choice and he commits himself to the others, he carries responsibility for the success of the group. The leader then becomes a facilitator, not the group "owner."

From *The Whole Person Survival Kit,* edited by Art Deyo (Youth for Christ/USA).

Okay, let's assume that you have the foundation—you know where the young people will come from. The next question to answer is this: why would kids want to get involved in a small group anyway? Of course, some kids will do just about anything you say, out of loyalty and friendship. They will go to the concert or camp, get into a small group, and even discuss boring topics if you ask them to. Usually, however, kids will need a better reason to get involved; they will need to be motivated. Here are some possible motivational links for most teenagers:

● They want to be with THEIR friends.

- They want to talk.
- They want to belong.
- They want to find answers to THEIR questions.
- They want to meet THEIR needs.
- They want to explore THEIR interests.

In addition, specific types of young people will have special reasons to get involved:

- Hurting kids will want help and support.
- New believers will want information and guidance in the Christian life.
- Growing Christians will want instruction.
- Student leaders will want training.
- Lonely kids will want relationships.

Remember these motives as you plan your small groups.

Leaders

Another crucial ingredient to the success of any small group is the leader, the person responsible for organizing the group and making sure that it works. Before beginning your small group ministry, therefore, you should think about who the group leaders will be. Do you have enough potential leaders already involved in the ministry, or will you have to recruit some?

The types of leaders that you will need will depend on the kinds of groups you want and your expectations for those groups—in other words, your "purpose" and "philosophy." (Note: How to lead small groups is dealt with in chapter 4.) And you will have to decide whether your potential leaders need any special training or experience. If the purpose of a group is to discuss difficult questions about the Bible and about the Christian life, the leader should have a certain level of Bible knowledge and some skill in leading discussions. A support group for kids from terrible home situations will need a leader who has knowledge of family systems and counseling. And remember that the most effective leaders will be those who already have good relationships with the kids in their groups.

High school students can also be small group leaders, but be careful who you ask them to lead and what you want them

LEADERSHIP

Without adequate leadership a small group is doomed. Groups can compensate for some deficiencies and frustrations, and still have a healthy life together. But without wise, loving leadership, a group will suffer from an inhibited beginning, stunted growth and accelerated demise. And who needs that?

Good leadership unlocks a small group's potential. A good music conductor guides the orchestra into producing harmony. A football quarterback coordinates the team with a specific play to score a touchdown. So the leader of a small group helps members clarify their purpose and reach it. With a good leader people will take off their masks and find the freedom to give and receive love.

From a chapter entitled "Leadership—The Critical Factor" by Doug Whallen, *Good Things Come in Small Groups* (InterVarsity Press, 1985), page 38.

to accomplish. Upperclassmen with mature and growing faith can effectively disciple new Christians, lead Bible studies, organize for service, and reach their friends for Christ. Don't assume that leaders must be adults. On the other hand, don't expect students to do more than they are able.

Be careful about who you choose as leaders—these men and women play a crucial role in the ministry because they touch kids directly.

THE MIX

After gathering the ingredients, the next step is mixing them together. With small group ministry, this means deciding who should be in which group. It involves choosing the kids who need the group, those who will fit in, and those who will move the group in the right direction. This process will be easy if the groups are formed to meet specific needs (e.g. a support group for kids of divorce, a follow-up course for new Christians, a group of those going on a missions trip, etc.). However, other types of small groups will be more tricky. Here are some factors to consider:

- relationships (Do these kids know the leader and each other?)
- personalities (Will the group get along?)
- similarities/differences (Do you want the group to be homogeneous or heterogeneous in age, culture, background, etc.?)
- needs/maturity (Will everyone be moving in the same direction?)
- geography (Do the kids live near each other or is transportation available?)

The correct answers to those questions depend on the purposes of the group. For example, if one of your goals is to break down cliques and establish new friendships in your youth group, you will want each small group to consist of kids who aren't already close friends. If your goal is to train student leaders, you will want kids who are fairly mature in their faith and motivated to serve. If the emphasis is on fellowship and community, you may want each group to have a variety of backgrounds, ages, and cultures.

It's also important to think through how you will "recruit" members of each small group. In this regard, you should consider the "ingredients" and the motives that we discussed earlier.

Years ago in YFC we had LUG groups. LUG stood for "Living Unit Group," and each group leader was called a "lughead." When I heard about the program, I couldn't wait to get my kids involved. So at an Insight meeting I explained to everyone what LUG was and how they could sign up after the meeting. But when I looked at the sign-up sheet, I found only a couple of names. My recruitment would have been much more effective if I had announced the program, and then, instead of having them sign up, I had invited kids personally, individually.

Of course what you and the other leaders say to individuals

THE WRONG MIX

"Since God's family includes people of all ages and backgrounds, so should our group." This attitude, laudable as it may be, can end up "firing the bullet" of the wrong mix. The issue here is *composition*.

Groups that merge all types and ages of people can work, but in the long run they often don't. Unless members already have strong social bonds, such as in a very small church, most people will simply feel uncomfortable in a group with others who do not share their interests and experiences.

On the other hand, groups that try too hard to be homogeneous can fall into the trap of exclusivism. Members can be so familiar with each other that the group lacks a healthy stimulation from within. A group of people who are all alike can be the wrong mix too.

From "Six Small Group Killers" by Neal McBride, *Discipleship Journal,* September/October, 1990.

to get them into groups will be determined to a great extent by the type of group(s) you want to organize. This will be covered later (in the last half of this book) when you can take a close look at a variety of successful, small group ministries. If you were organizing a small group for discipling new Christians, then, to each person, you might say something like: "I'm forming a small group of kids who have recently accepted Christ, and I'd like you to be a part of that group. We'll get together for an hour once a week, for six weeks, to answer questions, discuss issues, and talk about the first steps in the Christian life. This Saturday morning, we're going to meet at my house to get organized. Can you make it?"

If you wanted to use a small group to help build relationships with non-Christian kids, you would share your vision with a student leader. Then you would ask him or her to pull together some friends (both sexes) to form a group that would get together to "talk things over—everything from guys/girls to the occult—whatever they want to talk about."

Put the groups together carefully and prayerfully. You need the right ingredients and the right mix.

THE STIR

Okay, let's assume that you are the group leader and that you have talked individually with seven kids. They've agreed to meet with you this Saturday morning. What's next? How do you get started?

First, choose a non-threatening place to meet—one of the kid's homes, or, if they know you well, at your house. Offer to pick up those that you sense may find a last-second excuse not to come.

PERSON TO PERSON

It is clear that students will begin to listen to us only when they can begin to believe we are interested in them personally—as persons—and not merely as "things to be educated" (which is sometimes what the term "students" means to teachers).

However, if they can believe that I, as their discussion leader, am genuinely interested in them, that I would like to help them make sense out of some of the things that are puzzling them, they may begin to listen to me, and to accept me. If I can communicate to them the fact that I have no intention of forcing truths upon them or of packing my values into their minds, then we have a good chance of being able to work together.

From "Concern: A Discussion Series," Leader's Guide, by Rev. Andre Auw (Silver Burdett Company, 1970), page 4.

As kids arrive, greet them warmly, thank them for coming, and offer them refreshments. Background music will also help put everyone at ease. If the group consists of good friends, then conversation will flow naturally and smoothly. But you will have to take the initiative with those who don't know each other very well, making introductions and beginning conversations.

After everyone has come, seat them in a circle, on the same level if possible, (i.e., all in chairs or all on the floor, etc.), and make sure that they're comfortable. Begin by thanking them for coming. Then reiterate why you called the meeting and the purpose of the group: to get to know each other better and to _____. Explain that you want to meet for about an hour a week for six weeks, after which they can decide if they want to continue.

Also explain your role: leader, facilitator, guide, fellow member of the group, etc., but NOT a "teacher." They

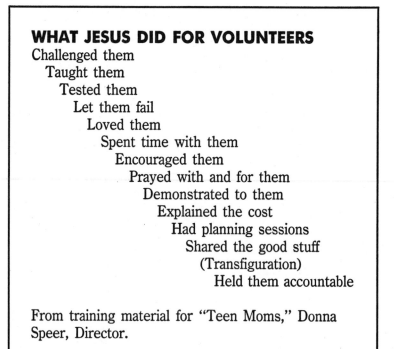

WHAT JESUS DID FOR VOLUNTEERS
Challenged them
  Taught them
    Tested them
      Let them fail
        Loved them
          Spent time with them
            Encouraged them
              Prayed with and for them
                Demonstrated to them
                  Explained the cost
                    Had planning sessions
                      Shared the good stuff
                      (Transfiguration)
                        Held them accountable

From training material for "Teen Moms," Donna Speer, Director.

should understand that the meetings will not be "classes" or "seminars."

Ask for questions and reactions. If they buy into the concept, decide on the best time and place for everyone to meet. Depending on the group and the purpose, you could meet at your house every week, at a different young person's house each time, in the church, or even in a restaurant. Some groups meet on weekday mornings, before school. Others meet on Sunday afternoons, weekday evenings, Saturday mornings, etc. Give suggestions, but let these be group decisions.

Next, spend some time getting to know each other better. If the kids aren't close friends, have each one tell about his or her family, place of birth, previous residence, etc. Then you could go around the circle with each person answering a non-threatening question such as: What is your idea of the perfect meal? What do you like best about your school; what do you hate? What's your favorite room in your house and why? And so forth. You can go a little deeper if you'd like, but keep this first meeting relatively light so that no one feels threatened.

End by telling them what to expect next. If you are going through lessons or a Bible study, make sure that everyone has the material and knows what to do before you get together again. Or you may want to give everyone an assignment, something to do, information to gather, etc., for the next meeting. Then, if it's appropriate, close in prayer.

The recipe for successful small group ministry begins with thinking through your purpose, philosophy, and plan; gathering the ingredients and mixing them with care; and stirring. But that's just the beginning. Next we must consider what happens in the mix—group dynamics.

THREE
ADDITION, MULTIPLICATION... AND DIVISION
Understanding Group Dynamics

How good are you at math? Here are a few easy problems to test your skill.

1. Two plus two equal _____?
2. Two times two equal _____?
3. Three apples plus one apple equal _____ apples?
4. Three people plus one person equal _____ relationships?

I told you the problems would be quick and easy. The answer to the first three is four. The fourth problem however, is a trick question, and it betrays a common misconception about small groups. You see, people cannot be dropped like apples into the equation, adding just one more relationship with each new person. Instead, relationships multiply, with the total growing quickly with each addition.

Suppose, for example, there are just two people, Gregg and Robert, two friends. That's one relationship to maintain. But if Ken joins them, suddenly there are four relationships to consider: Gregg and Robert, Gregg and Ken, Robert and Ken, and all three together. Enter Tom, and the relationship total jumps to ten—four people in various configurations of twos and threes, and all four together. If you're not sure about this, watch the chemistry as kids mix at your next Sunday School class or youth group meeting, and the reactions in various combinations of students. Young people will act differently depending on who is in the group.

People and relationships are not as simple as apples (or numbers). Each person has his or her own unique blend of personal history, character, values, personality, abilities, and other characteristics. When mixed with other breathing, thinking, and feeling persons, there is communication and interaction. People connect, and there is "relationship." Can you imagine how many relationships are possible in a group of eight? I won't even venture a guess, but it's a bunch!

We must understand, therefore, that we cannot simply bring six to ten kids together and expect to have a great small group experience, just because everyone's together. Small group ministry is much more than dividing into groups — that's just the beginning. There are many other "human" factors to consider. The most important of these is GROUP DYNAMICS, and that's what we'll discuss in this chapter.

ENERGY

In it's root form, the word "dynamic" means "energy" or "force." So "group dynamics" refers to the forces and energy within the circle of people who are meeting together — the action and interaction in a group.

A number of factors affect how each individual will relate with others. These include the person's background, personality, problems, friendships in the group, self-concept, age, and many others. Imagine, for example, how each of these high school students would react in a group discussing dating.

- Jason: sophomore, shy, average looking, never gone on a date, finds it difficult to talk to girls
- Tricia: junior, cheerleader, popular, extrovert, is going with Trent — the football team captain and a senior
- Jerome: junior, friendly, funny, Trent's friend but would love to go out with Tricia
- Allyson: freshman, cute, isn't allowed to date yet, flirts with all the boys, talkative

SMALL GROUP ADVANTAGES AND DISADVANTAGES

Advantages:
1. Young people like to do things together in groups.
2. A group is socially acceptable.
3. There are some activities that only small groups can do.
4. Small groups provide opportunities for communication.

Disadvantages:
1. Relationships multiply rapidly.
2. Personalities often clash.
3. Individuals can sometimes dominate or intimidate.
4. People "play" social "games."

From *Youth Evangelism* by David Veerman (Victor Books, 1988), pages 131-134.

- Michael: quiet, depressed lately, recently split with Sandi, parents just separated, hates school
- Neil: handsome, personable, a real ladies' man, has dated both Tricia and Sandi
- Sandi: serious about her relationship with God, broke up with Michael for spiritual reasons, straight-A student
- Francine: senior, good-looking, recently moved to town, had an abortion two years ago that no one here knows about, just started coming to church
- Caroline: also a cheerleader and Tricia's best friend, comes to the group to see Neil, is not a Christian

You might be saying, "Hey, that's my youth group, and I remember that meeting, what a disaster!"

Seriously, what do you think might be going on beneath the surface of each individual as you begin the discussion? How might certain people react to others as the meeting progresses? How honest would each person be?

I have described this imaginary group to give you an idea of the factors that affect group dynamics. And my descriptions are not that far-fetched. Often more diverse groups than that are assembled and are successful.

FACTORS

No group contains a collection of perfectly compatible personalities, all honest and vulnerable people, with spiritual depth and an overwhelming desire to do God's will. So don't expect that. Instead, realize that what happens in your group will be affected by many factors. Let's take a closer look.

Felt Needs

These are pressing concerns for each individual. A person's needs could be emotional and psychological (e.g., feeling lonely, feeling unloved, wondering about identity, feeling guilty, etc.), social (e.g., needing a friend, needing a date, etc.), and mental (e.g., having serious questions about life, God, the future, etc.). These needs are right at the surface and can become the person's hidden agenda in a meeting. For example, someone who needs attention may continually change the subject or interrupt the discussion with a joke.

Personal Crises

These are similar to felt needs because they are pressing for resolution now. Teenage crises could include having parents who are fighting, separating, or divorcing; breaking up with a boyfriend or girlfriend (or being dumped by him or her); struggling with an injury or sickness; losing something valuable; failing a class; being cut from a team; fighting with a friend; and so forth. Again, if a person is experiencing crisis, it will be difficult for him or her to concentrate on anything else. And this person may overreact to a slight provocation.

Background

The way a person has been treated in the past will affect how he or she acts in the present. Important elements in a person's history could include: family dynamics and values, per-

PERSONALITY CONFLICTS

When pilgrims travel together, they're bound to learn a lot about each other. But they won't always like what they learn! Some pilgrims are too talkative and domineering; others are too critical or dramatic; some lack commitment to the pilgrim group and are always late. Friction is inevitable.

Don't be afraid of problems between pilgrims! Crises are opportunities for growth. That's why you join a pilgrim group—to grow. It's true that small groups often bring out personality problems, but they also provide one of the best places for working those problems out. Problems are a normal part of growing together—even a necessary part. Problems shouldn't be surprising since all of us who come together in groups are needy people. Use problems the way God intended—as a means toward growth.

From *Pilgrims in Progress* by Jim and Carol Plueddemann (Harold Shaw Publishers, 1990), pages 85-86.

sonal experiences, education, Christian knowledge and commitment, and many others. Some people really think they know everything, and will act like it in a group. Others may come from a very conservative background and feel threatened by group honesty.

Personality

These are the qualities or traits that make the individual distinctive, especially in how he or she relates to others. Personality characteristics include: outgoing, shy, funny, serious, rowdy, thoughtful, quick, effervescent, dull, eager, talkative, quiet, lazy, perceptive, disciplined, aggressive, flighty, focused, antagonistic, steady, ambitious, happy, animated, persistent, sensitive, loving—and on and on. Each person has his or her own special combination.

Interpersonal History

This is simply what has happened previously between and among group members. If some of the kids go to the same school or live in the same neighborhood, they will already have a "pecking order," an informal hierarchy of status and influence. Some group members may be best friends and others, competitive rivals. And in a co-ed group, there are always romantic overtones. This can lead to subtle put-downs or making statements to make an impression.

Other factors to consider are age, maturity, knowledge, and experience in other small groups.

As I said in chapter 2, your purpose for your small groups will affect the general mix of kids in each group. But even a group with seemingly everything in common will have a kaleidoscope of differences. Obviously, if handled wrong, any number of these factors could thwart a group's process and progress and even throw a meeting into chaos. All of these factors make any group unpredictable. But don't be dismayed; they also can give a group energy and make it dynamic. The differences among group members can be an advantage by:

- challenging pat answers—making a person explain his or her cliches. I grew up in a strong Christian home and church. I knew all the right answers to say in Sunday School and at youth group. It would have been helpful for someone from another church to ask me what "born again" and "separation" meant.
- bringing new information—shedding light on a problem or question. A rich variety of family, church, and geographical backgrounds can provide fresh insights. Group members can learn from each other. Because my friend told me what he went through when his dad died, I was better prepared for my own father's death.
- broadening perspectives—seeing life from another point of view. Because Campus Life was an interdenominational ministry, kids from the whole spectrum of Christendom came to the club. This made for exciting discussions at our

Insight meetings because kids couldn't predict how those from other churches would answer. The variety of religious experiences helped each person see from a broader vantage point.

MAKING GROUP DYNAMICS POSITIVE

There are three components for making group dynamics positive. With these you can transform differences in the group from liabilities to assets. The necessary components are *awareness, atmosphere,* and *attitude.*

Awareness

The first component in managing group dynamics is being aware that the differences exist and that much is going on beneath the surface. Then you won't be surprised when something bursts out into the open. Since you have read the first half of this chapter, you are aware of the types of differences that can be found in any group. In addition, it is invaluable to be aware of what the *specific* differences and dynamics are. To do that, you have to know your kids.

There is no substitute for building relationships with youth outside of the youth group and ministry programs. And the more time you spend with someone and the stronger your friendship becomes, the more you will know about that person. You can build these friendships by making campus visits, attending school events, driving kids to games, going out for Cokes, etc. Today the students in our school district have the day off. And right now, as I write this, my 15-year-old daughter is at the mall with a member of the high school ministry team from church. They're going to lunch and then shopping. A friendship is being built.

Be sure to mention at your small group meetings and at other events that you are also available to talk, one-on-one. Kids will open up during these individual discussions and counseling sessions. Your awareness of what kids are going through will help you head off problems and guide discussions in a beneficial and healthy direction.

I remember a group of upperclassmen guys with whom I

met regularly to talk about life in general, and to work on Christian discipleship in particular. Because of my relationship with Craig, I knew that his father was an alcoholic. In fact, Craig and I had talked several times about how his father was destroying the family. So when our group began to discuss God as our Heavenly Father, I suggested to the group that some people find it difficult to love God because of problems with their earthly fathers. When they hear "Heavenly *Father*," they have a very negative image. Then we discussed what God as a perfect Father is like. Knowing Craig's family life helped me to be sensitive to him, and helped me guide the group.

In this regard, be careful not to violate confidences. Don't share with the group information that someone has told you confidentially, in private. But what you know about the specific individuals will help you lead the group in a positive direction. In addition, you will be sensitive to how a person might feel when discussing a certain topic, and you will understand why someone reacted the way he or she did. And in private conversations, you may want to encourage some individuals to open up and share secrets, hidden facts, or deep feelings with the whole group.

Parents are also a great source of information. They know their kids better than anyone else and may be willing to tell you about their son or daughter's personality, pressures, and problems. I remember a father explaining that his son was dyslexic. This helped me understand why he had struggled in school and why he was reluctant to read aloud in our group. Special note: It's always important to communicate with parents continually in every type of youth ministry, and this goes double for small group leaders. Parents want to know this person who is spending so much time with their child. (I speak as a concerned parent.)

Even if Mom and/or Dad doesn't share any inside information, you can learn much about a young person by just going to the house, seeing where he or she lives, and meeting the rest of the family.

Awareness is the first and most important component for helping you manage group dynamics.

Atmosphere

The second component is the environment of your small group meetings, or "atmosphere." It's important for kids to feel comfortable and accepted. This begins with the physical environment. The small group isn't a class, so kids shouldn't sit in desks or in rows. And it isn't church, so stay away from pews. Instead, sit on the carpeted floor, on cushions, or in comfortable chairs and couches.

A few years ago, I noticed that in some of my Campus Life meetings, crowd control was a breeze—everyone cooperated and participated. At other meetings (for the same school), however, the crowd was rowdy and hard to handle. As a staff, we analyzed every aspect of the situation, including the games we played, the topics we discussed, and the kids who came. But no pattern emerged. Then after a particularly boistrous meeting, the answer hit us. It was what was *underneath*. In all of our meetings, we had kids sit on the floor. Whenever they sat on carpet, they acted great; but when they sat on tile, they gave us a hard time. Because they were uncomfortable on the tile, they moved around a lot, were impatient, and bugged their neighbors. The environment made the difference.

Not only will comfort enhance group participation, it will also defuse potentially explosive reactions. It's more difficult to be angry when you feel good.

It's also important, however, not to allow the group to become TOO comfortable. Avoid overstuffed, easy chairs where kids sink in and lay back. You don't want anyone falling asleep or pulling back from the discussion.

It is wise to have the group sit in a circle, on the same level, so that there can be eye contact. This will encourage everyone to participate. In other words, don't have one person sitting back in an easy chair, someone sitting on the floor in front of him, someone else lying down at the side, and someone "hiding" behind the couch. Members should feel as though they are all on equal footing in the group. And remember, you should be in the circle too.

Lighting is also important. The room should be well lit, but not too bright. Indirect lighting is best. This will add to the relaxed, comfortable feel and help everyone see each other.

Also remove all potential distractions. This means having the television and radio off, pets out of the room, and little brothers and sisters away from the group. Refreshments are okay as long as they don't distract. Popcorn, chips, and M & Ms seem to work well.

Obviously, each potential setting has advantages and disadvantages. If you meet in a restaurant, try to get a room or a distant corner to yourselves. If you meet in a home, let your host know what you expect regarding pets, TV, siblings, etc.

There's something else that is vital for building a positive environment. It's intangible and more difficult to control than the physical aspects of a room, and seating arrangements. But it's the most important ingredient—*acceptance*. Kids should know that the group is SAFE, that they will not be put down, and will be accepted for who they are.

Acceptance begins with you, the leader. Think about how you greet each person. They should believe that you are thrilled that they have come and that the group just wouldn't be the same without them. And as the leader, it is your responsibility to insure that group members value acceptance of everyone, and work at it. As you organize the group, explain that put-downs and gossip are not allowed and that everything said in the group stays there. The group is a place where they can be themselves and can be honest, without fear of anything they say being used against them.

A positive atmosphere will help group members be positive. They will tend to cooperate and not let differences divide them.

Attitude

The final component for managing group dynamics and using differences to your advantage is the group process itself, including the way you lead, the way you encourage members to relate to each other, and the ground rules for your discussions. This means building a positive and healthy group attitude. Here's how.

● Honesty—Let everyone know that they can be honest about what they feel and think. If they don't agree, they

RULES
(WHAT MAKES THE GROUP WORK?)

One of the key factors to make the group work is the three rules that all group members and the leader follow. These rules help the leader build an environment in which honest sharing and learning will take place. The rules are:

1. BE HONEST OR BE SILENT. The group will never force anyone to share. An individual is always allowed to not answer. Silence becomes a form of honesty by simply saying "I'm not willing to be honest on that yet." The group is continually challenged to share at more honest levels. Three levels of honesty are talked about. The levels are *honest, more honest,* and *most honest.*

2. BE TOTALLY CONFIDENTIAL. Practicing confidentiality is the only way anything of importance and honesty can be shared by the group. Sharing things outside the group which are shared within may cause someone to no longer be allowed in the group. Trust is vital.

3. BE COMMITTED TO COMING TO THE MEETING. The commitment of the group members to each other will make this a special time each week.

The rules must be communicated to the group often. The leader must be careful to follow the rules. The communication of the rules will remind the group and give the group confidence in them.

From *Honest to God* by Dave Bartlett (Youth for Christ/USA, 1989), pages 3-4.

should say so. If they have questions, they should ask them. If they feel angry, sad, frustrated, fearful, etc., they should let the group know. Be sure, however, to temper this honesty with sensitivity. Explain that no one is allowed to blast or dump on anyone else.

● Respect—Explain that in any group, there will be honest differences of opinion. Not everyone will agree on everything all the time. So while they should be free to express their opinions honestly, they should also be aware that others may disagree, and may say so. Although not everyone's opinion will be right (correct), everyone will have the right to his or her opinion. There should be a healthy give and take. Also let them know that they can disagree with *you* and that they may ask questions that you can't answer. Then you all will look for the answers together.

AFFIRM, ACCEPT, ENCOURAGE

Here's what leaders can do to provide affirmation, acceptance, and encouragement in a group.

● Provide all members with a roster, including birthdays.

● Use every occasion to celebrate! Start in the fall with a kick-off that sets the tone for the year. Celebrate birthdays and holidays. End the year with a spring celebration party.

● Express caring with small birthday gifts, such as decorated sacks filled with inexpensive items and printed on the outside with a caring message.

● Contact members frequently.

From "Fresh Ideas" by Becky Teter, *Discipleship Journal,* September/October, 1990, page 26.

It is also important for group members to know that each person in the group is unique—and special (as we discussed at the beginning of this chapter). They should respect those differences. You don't expect everyone to be the same.

● Affirmation—As the group leader, look for ways to affirm each young person in the group, each time you meet. Compliment them on doing the assignment, thank them for their answers and insights, praise them for being such good listeners, etc. Don't be phony with this and stretch the truth or make stuff up; look for genuine opportunities to affirm.

● Commitment—At your first meeting, try to get everyone to promise to meet faithfully for a set number of weeks (e.g., six). Each time you get together, remind them of your commitment to each other. Explain that if the group is frustrating to them, isn't meeting their expectations, or is going in the wrong direction, they should let you know, so you can work together on improving the situation. But they shouldn't just stop coming. Explain also that, hopefully, their commitment will be to the group and the other members, and not to just meeting a certain number of times.

In any group of human beings, there will be a multitude of differences, with strong potential for conflict, confrontation, and confusion. But these differences can also be positive, providing opportunities for growth. To take advantage of them, however, involves awareness and sensitivity, a positive and comfortable atmosphere, and a healthy group attitude. And the reason for much of the success of any group is leadership. That's you. And that's what the next chapter is about.

FOUR
THE LEADING EDGE
Finding and Training Small Group Leaders

What characteristic do all of the following people have in common?

Saddam Hussein	Billy Graham
Elizabeth Dole	Jesse Jackson
Margaret Thatcher	Dwight D. Eisenhower
Mother Theresa	Attila the Hun
Hammer	Michael Jordan
Carmen Sandiego	Martin Luther King, Jr.
Fidel Castro	Paul the Apostle
Barbara Bush	

The answer? All are (or were) leaders. We know they are leaders because they have had a following. Whether for good or evil, they lead (or led) people. The leadership styles for this unusual collection vary greatly: some were elected to leadership positions; some lead (led) by force; some by performance; some by the power of their personalities; and others by example.

I have also seen a wide variety of leadership styles in youth ministry. Some youth leaders were appointed to the position, hired by the church to work with the high school students. Others are charismatic leaders; that is, they draw kids like the fabled Pied Piper. And others simply dig in and work, forging a loyal following by winning the respect of young people and their parents.

But what kind of style will be most effective in small group leadership? What is the profile of the ideal small group leader? Those are good questions without simple answers. In fact, it's impossible to profile a person who would be guaranteed success with *any* group. That's because individuals and groups are so different (we looked at the variables in the last chapter), and each group has its own, distinct personality. Of course, certain groups will need specific types of leaders because of their special focuses (as we discussed in Chapter 2), but there is no ideal profile. One thing is sure, however, small group leaders DO NOT have to have:

- charisma—extreme good looks and personal charm
- power—influence in the church, community, or school
- public speaking or teaching skills
- outstanding physical ability
- a certain age, race, or sex

QUALITIES

To get a better idea of what a small group leader should be like, let's take a close look at what he or she is expected to do. Remember, our definition of a small group is: "a group of about 4–10 young people and a leader who meet together regularly and are committed to each other, to the group, and to learning and growing together."

Because the small group leader will be expected to relate with kids, he or she should have *interpersonal skills*. The small group leader doesn't have to be an extrovert or a comedian, but he or she should be friendly, warm, and sincere, someone that a young person could consider a "good friend."

Because the group will "meet together regularly," the small group leader should be *organized and disciplined*. He or she will have to schedule meetings, communicate with group members, and be on time.

LEADERSHIP

Good leadership can make a major contribution to the healthy development of pilgrims, and bad leadership can do tremendous harm. Leadership style cannot be based merely on the preference of the leader or the follower. Some people prefer unhealthy leadership styles.

From *Pilgrims in Progress* by Jim and Carol Plueddemann (Harold Shaw Publishers, 1990), page 66.

Because the group will meet "to learn and grow together," the small group leader should have *communication skills*. This simply means the ability to carry on a conversation and to lead a discussion. I will cover how to lead a discussion in chapter 5.

Because group members are "committed to each other," the small group leader should be *willing to spend time* outside of meetings with individuals, building relationships, counseling, and being a friend.

Because the group is in the context of Christian ministry, the small group leader should be solid in *Christian commitment* and growing in the faith.

As I think of some of the volunteers who led small groups for me over the years, I remember a shy college girl, a stay-at-home mother, a carpenter contractor, a salesman, a physical education teacher, a lawyer, and others. They had a wide variety of occupations, educations, and personalities. And most were effective leaders.

Earlier I said that small group leaders are not "teachers." By this I mean they should not see their primary task as imparting information, as in presenting a seminar or giving a lecture. Doubtless, learning will take place in the small groups; the content covered in each meeting is very important. But group members should feel that they are learning together. So a better title for describing the role of a small group leader would be "facilitator" or "guide." The leader is a friend and coach who comes alongside group members and helps them grow in the right direction.

That description should help you see how effective you might be in leading a small group, and in looking for other, potential small group leaders.

ACTION

Let's assume, then, that you've discovered and recruited leaders for your small groups. Next we turn to how that person actually leads the group, what he or she does in a small group meeting.

Again, there is not a step by step process that a leader should follow each time a group gets together. What happens at a small group meeting will be determined for the most part by the purpose of the group, the members of the group, and the material to be covered. But there are four types of action that the leader should take to be effective.

Lead

The small group leader should lead. This isn't as obvious as it sounds because I've just said that each small group leader should be more like a friend than a teacher. And the leader should be seen as a group member, sitting in the circle with everyone else, not standing or positioned above and in front of them. But there is a leadership function that the leader must assume. His or her task includes more than calling the meeting and convening the group. That's why earlier I described the leader as a "facilitator" or "guide."

First, the small group leader leads by *giving direction*. This includes helping the group set goals and outlining the necessary steps to reach those goals. At the initial meeting of a small group of new Christians who are meeting to study the basics of the Christian life, the leader might say something like: "The goal of our meetings is to learn about the Christian life, what God wants us to know, and how He wants us to

---

WHAT THE SMALL GROUP LEADER DOES

Someone in the small group has to serve by initiating and guiding. Especially in the early stages of the group's life, the leader plays a crucial role in helping the group establish a direction and gain momentum. The designated leader usually serves the small group by:

1. Providing sense of purpose and vision.
2. Initiating activities.
3. Encouraging others.
4. Setting expectations.
5. Organizing logistics.

From a chapter entitled "Leadership—The Critical Factor" by Doug Whallon, *Good Things Come in Small Groups* (InterVarsity Press, 1985), page 42.

---

live. To do that, we will be going through this book, *First Steps,* together . . . ."

Second, the small group leader leads by *keeping the group on track.* In any gathering of friends there is a time for small talk. And if a group is successful, relationships will develop to the point where individuals will share some of their deep concerns, regardless of what's on the agenda for that meeting. So by "keeping the group on track" I don't mean being all business, or shutting down serious sharing. But there will be times when the leader will have to pull the group back together and head them in the same direction again.

Let's say that in a discussion about dating, Martha begins to tell everyone about a frustrating date she had a few months before. She is being honest and is making an important point. In her explanation, Martha gives the title of the movie she saw that night. At that point Gwen interrupts and begins talking about that particular movie, how she didn't like it, and so forth. Then Sheri chimes in with her movie review.

That's an example of when the leader should bring the group back to the topic at hand.

At other times (e.g., continual interrupting, two or three kids talking at the same time, inappropriate humor, put-downs) the leader may have to stop and remind the group of the ground rules for the discussions and the purpose of the group. If the leader doesn't take leadership in this area, the group will fall apart.

Keeping the group on track may also mean defusing anger and resolving conflicts between members. Hopefully others in the group will also be peacemakers, but the responsibility falls on the leader.

Third, the small group leader leads by *asking good questions* and *probing for answers*. (See chapter 5 for more on leading discussions.) A good small group leader encourages members to be honest and helps them think through their answers.

IT ISN'T ALWAYS EASY

Leading a small group can be devastating. We've all been with kids in a small group when no one speaks or when one person monopolized the entire conversation.

Leading a small group takes a certain amount of skill that may not come easily.

From *The Youth Builder* by Jim Burns (Harvest House, 1988), pages 126-127.

People are used to relating on a superficial level and talking in cliches: "Hi, how are ya?" "Fine." "How's it goin'?" "Great!" And kids learn to answer their parents and other adults with quick, one-word answers: "How was school today?" "Good." Sometimes it seems like too much work to think things through and to answer from the heart. The leader has to take the initiative here, carefully framing the questions and asking "Why?"

The small group leader should lead by giving direction, keeping the group on track, and asking good questions.

Listen

Remember asking a person a question, but having to repeat it because he wasn't listening? And remember telling a friend about something that happened; while you were talking, she was looking around the room? Or how about the time you told someone how you felt about an issue, but he totally missed your point? Nothing is more frustrating than having something to say and having no one to listen. The small group should be a place where kids share what's really on their minds and hearts, and people listen.

The small group leader should be that kind of person — a listener.

I've been in discussions where the leader would ask a question but really didn't want an answer. Instead, he was using the question as a platform for his next statement. And so instead of listening to what was said in response, the leader was forming his next sentence in his mind, waiting for his chance to speak.

Once, in discussing the book of Revelation, the leader asked for everyone's views of "the end times." Before everyone could answer, however, he jumped in and presented his personal prophetic view.

In contrast, good small group leaders listen intently to what is said, carefully thinking through each person's statements.

Listening to others shows that we value them as persons; we think they have something important to say and something valuable to contribute — to us and to the group. By listening, the group leader affirms the speaker and models to group members how they should respond to each other.

There are four steps to good listening:

1. The listener should lean slightly toward the person who is speaking. This shows that he or she is concentrating on what the speaker is saying.
2. The listener should make eye contact with the speaker. This makes the communication personal and shows that the listener cares about the speaker as a person.

3. The listener should think about what the person is saying. This will help him or her focus on the speaker's message.
4. After the person has finished talking, the listener should reflect back what he or she thinks the person said (e.g., "I hear you saying that you really hate school." "It sounds like he really hurt you."). This shows that the listener really was listening and wants to make sure that he or she understands what the speaker said and meant.

THE LEADER

The leader is an equal participant in the group. Members of the group will look to the leader as they decide how honest, vulnerable, and open they will be. By example, the leader will teach members how to listen and care. The leader's faith will be caught!

The leader must be: learning, praying, enthusiastic, honest, vulnerable, confident, and flexible.

From *Honest to God* by Dave Bartlett (Youth for Christ/USA, 1989), pages 4-5.

Some people seem to think that discussion leaders should do all the talking; so whenever there's a lull, they fill the silence with talk or quickly move to the next question. The silence may mean that people are thinking, or it may mean that the question was bad. Leading involves much more than asking and talking; it also involves listening.

Learn

Good small group leaders are good learners. As the meeting progresses, the leader who listens and watches carefully can learn a lot about group members.

Dennis became very silent when the discussion turned to family life. Sonia seemed to be defensive in her response to Carin. Michelle's eyes looked very sad and she could hardly look at anyone.

By watching for verbal and non-verbal clues, the leader may uncover a hidden hurt or fear, head off a potential conflict, or see a new side to a person. This may help the leader guide the discussion, or it may propel him or her to seek out an individual after the meeting.

In addition to learning *about* group members, the leader can learn *from* them. Good leaders realize that they don't have all the answers and that people in the group can teach them a thing or two.

During my second year of youth ministry (which seems like aeons ago), one of my fellow staff members told me: "I will be open to learning from you if I think you can learn from me." His message was clear: I was always ready to give advice, but I wasn't open to receiving any.

Respect and honesty go both ways. If we want kids to be honest and to respect us, then we should be honest and respect them. This means listening to what they have to say and learning from them. Group meetings should be learning experiences for everyone, including the leader.

SELECTION OF ADULT LEADERS

Each group has a young adult leader who has committed himself to the students. These leaders are carefully chosen on the basis of their Christian commitment, their love for students, and their ability to relate well. They are not there to lecture, but to facilitate discussion, to interact with students, to foster an atmosphere conducive to spiritual growth, and to make themselves available for personal counsel and guidance.

From a chapter entitled "Ministering through Core Groups" by John Musselman, *The Youth Leader's Source Book,* Gary Dausey, editor (Zondervan Publishing House, 1983), page 145.

Love

Many people wonder what makes great youth ministers successful. Youth leaders come in all shapes and sizes, with many different combinations of skills and gifts. But the common denominator for the great ones is love. They love their kids. I don't mean they have warm or romantic feelings about them (let's face it, some kids aren't too loveable). They love kids by acting loving toward them. And make no mistake, kids know when they're loved. They may not respond right away or say thanks, but they know.

The good small group leader shows love toward the individual members of the group.

Love means expressing concern about a situation, a problem, or an issue that comes up in a meeting. Love means affirming kids, and giving genuine compliments. Love means praying for group members—daily bringing their specific needs before the Father. Love means spending time with individuals outside of the meetings. Love means offering help, answers, and counsel. Love means introducing young people to Christ.

Be the kind of leader who is known for love, love that is sincere (Romans 12:9).

That's what it takes to be a good, small group leader. The profile wasn't very specific, but I think you get the picture. Besides having interpersonal skills, being organized and disciplined, having communication skills, being willing to spend time, and having a strong Christian commitment, good leaders LEAD, LISTEN, LEARN, and LOVE.

FIVE
TALKING IN CIRCLES
Leading Great Discussions

---

1. What's the best discussion you have ever been part of? (Give your answer aloud.)
2. Why did you have trouble answering question number one?

_____

_____

3. Why might someone say that the first question was a poor question to ask?

That was a feeble attempt to begin a chapter about discussions with a discussion. Unfortunately, however, that's what many discussions are—feeble attempts. The leader throws out a few questions, but everyone just sits there in embarrassed silence until some courageous soul ventures a response.

But discussions are the soul of effective small groups, with intriguing questions eliciting thoughtful responses, group members honestly sharing and interacting, and the leader gently probing and guiding.

What makes the difference? What makes discussions work? That's the focus of this chapter.

THE SEARCH FOR TRUTH

Dialogue is indispensable also in the search for truth, and here, too, it is a worker of miracles. Unfortunately, many people hold and proclaim what they believe to be true in either an opinionated or defensive way. Religious people, for example, sometimes speak the truth they profess monologically, that is, they hold it exclusively and inwardly as if there was no possible relation between what they believe and what others believe, in spite of every indication that separately held truths are often complementary. The monological thinker runs the danger of being prejudiced, intolerant, bigoted, and a persecutor of those who differ from him. The dialogical thinker, on the other hand, is willing to speak out of his convictions to the holders of other convictions with genuine interest in them and with a sense of the possibilities between them.

From *The Miracle of Dialogue* by Reuel L. Howe (The Seabury Press, 1963), pages 9–10.

PURPOSE

As we begin, it's important to understand the reasons for having discussions. Knowing the "whys" will help us with the "hows."

Togetherness

The essence of the small group experience is togetherness, and so in this book I've emphasized "meeting together" and "learning and growing together." That's what makes a small group session different from a class or seminar—not the size of the group but the feeling that the group is *together*—unified, committed, moving in the same direction. Members don't just "attend," they *belong*.

People feel that they are a part of a group when they have the chance to participate, answer, respond, interact, and speak their minds. They know they belong when their opinions are accepted and their ideas are valued.

That can't happen in silence, with individuals keeping their thoughts and feelings to themselves. And it can't happen when the communication is only one direction, from speaker to listener. There must be dialogue.

Discussions can bring a group together.

Communication

Discussion, meaning dialogue and feedback, is also necessary for effective communication. Often what is said is not what is heard.

For years I used the expression, "accept Christ as your personal Savior" to explain what it means to become a Christian. To me that was a clear, evangelistic statement of biblical truth. "Personal Savior" means that Jesus died for *you*, not just the impersonal "whole world." In fact, if you had been the only person on earth, He would have gone to the cross for your sins. And the phrase "accept Christ" reflects the truth that God doesn't force salvation on anyone; it's a gift that must be accepted by faith, and certainly is not earned. I thought that the statement was easily understandable, very appropriate, and much better than "saved" or "born again." But one day a minister took me to task, explaining, "We don't 'accept Christ,' He accepts us." And later, one of the students explained that for weeks she thought I was saying "*except* Christ," thus hearing a message opposite to what I had intended. Even the simplest sentence can be misunderstood.

One-way communication assumes that the listeners understand perfectly everything that is being said. Don't make that assumption; instead, engage in dialogue through discussion.

People need clarifications, expansions, illustrations, and explanations. Discussion helps people understand and find answers. Discussion also helps people know what others are thinking.

Discussions can help people communicate.

ENERGY

The average lecture/message/sermon is about as interesting as watching grass grow. The group member can listen much faster than the speaker can talk. So he slouches down in his chair, shifts into neutral, and passively lets the speaker's words wash over him. But discussion calls for response. It takes energy to figure out what you want to say in a constantly changing discussion. The heart begins to beat; the juices begin to flow. I'll be closed to new ideas as long as I can hang back and not express my thoughts. But if you can jog me into debating the merits of my opinion, I may start churning inside. Once my rigid views are thawed I might be willing to consider a different or even "wrong" position.

From *Getting Together, A Guide for Good Groups* by Dr. Em Griffin (InterVarsity Press, 1982), page 89.

Challenge

Open and honest discussion helps people think. After all, it's hard to remain silent when someone makes a statement with which you vehemently disagree. You want to challenge that person to back up the assertion, to give reasons. But you also know that your statements may be challenged as well, so you dig beneath the easy answers and clichés in your mind to what you really think and feel, before blurting out a superficial response.

After just two years of full-time youth ministry, I was asked to participate in a national task force, a "think tank" for brainstorming ideas and writing materials. I was flattered by the invitation, but I was somewhat intimidated when I realized who the other participants would be: men and women whose ministries I had admired and emulated. When the group met, at first I just listened, reluctant to contradict those ministry experts or to submit my ideas for evaluation. But as I watched and listened to them interact with candor and care, I gained courage and soon jumped into the verbal free-for-all. Not having my comments received as "pearls of wisdom" was painful at first, so I was defensive, taking each critique as a personal attack. But eventually I relaxed and became a participating member of the group. That was an exhilarating growth experience for me because I was accepted as a person of worth with something valuable to contribute, and because I was challenged to think and to defend my answers.

Discussions can bring a group together and can facilitate communication. And the honest give-and-take in every discussion can challenge individuals to think, evaluate, and grow.

PHILOSPHY
As we discussed in chapter 2, "philosophy" refers to the framework or the grid of the ministry. Another way to explain it is that these are the "ground rules" for the game, that everyone in the group (including the leader, must follow. Explain these rules to the group as you begin, and remind everyone of the rules again as the need arises.

Be Honest
If the group is to provide a place where individuals can learn and grow together, group members must be honest. This means expressing what they really think and feel, including doubts, challenges, and questions, and also fears, hurts, and misgivings. If the discussion is to be honest, however, everyone must agree to confidentiality. Group members should know that what they say will stay at the meeting, and not be spread around school or church. Confidentiality is a by-product of the group's commitment to each other.

KEEPING THE DISCUSSION GOING

At some point in one of the early sessions you should mention a few principles of effective communication, which can help to keep the discussion moving along and permit the students to share that responsibility with you. The following are some of the principles that should be shared.

- Remember that it's *our* discussion—yours and mine. We can make it good or bad.
- Learn to listen. Above all, learn to listen to the person behind the idea.
- Tell us not only what you think, tell us also how you feel about what you think.
- Respect the person speaking, even though you may disagree with his or her ideas or values.
- When in doubt, check it out! Make sure you understand what the person is saying before you criticize his or her opinion.
- Share your thoughts with us. Don't keep them to yourself.
- Let others carry the ball. Don't dominate a discussion and become a bore.
- Stick to the point, please. Allow us to remind you that you have wandered away from what we were talking about.
- Learn to listen. (That's repeated because it can't be overstressed, and we always have to be reminded of it.)

From the Leader's Guide for *Concern: a Discussion Series* by Rev. Andre Auw (Silver Burdett Company, 1970), page 9.

Be Accepting

If the group is to be the place where individuals can be totally honest with their thoughts and feelings, it must be a safe place where people won't be attacked or put down. This doesn't mean that no one can question what someone has said, or that everyone has to pretend agreement. If people are honest, there will be honest disagreements. But group members should accept and affirm the person even if they reject what he or she is saying.

Be Respectful

This also refers to how group members treat each other. In a discussion, respect is needed by both "giver" and "receiver." A disrespectful statement would be something like: "Anyone who thinks that way is stupid!" or using vulgarity or calling names. Respect means expressing oneself with care. Being respectful in a discussion also means allowing others to speak. Someone who dominates the discussion is acting as though he or she is the only one who has anything worthwhile to say. That's incorrect, and disrespectful.

For the receiver, showing respect means not interrupting, but really listening to what the giver is saying. It also means quietly thinking through all personal disagreements and potential challenges.

Honest, accepting, and respectful discussions do not have to be boring or sickeningly polite and proper (e.g., "I respectfully disagree with my esteemed collegue . . . "). They can be energetic, boisterous, free-flowing, and exciting. Group members should leave feeling challenged and energized—never beaten or put down.

PLAN

Seating

As I mentioned previously, the group should be seated in a circle (in chairs or on the floor) so that everyone is on the same level and there is eye contact. You (the leader) should be in the circle too. This will help each person feel part of the group and will enhance communication. Everyone should be comfortable, so avoid sitting on tile or cement floors or in hard chairs.

Leading

In the last chapter, we covered leadership, so this is just a brief reminder that as group leader, your main task is to be a facilitator or guide for the group. Nowhere will this be more important than in the discussions. Ask questions, state your ideas honestly, encourage everyone to get involved, keep the discussion moving, and end on time. Don't make speeches, belittle anyone's answer, play the role of the answer-person, bluff an answer, or get into an argument. Follow the discussion ground rules yourself, and remember the purposes for the discussion and for the group.

Getting Started

If, at the first meeting of the group, students don't know each other very well, begin by introducing yourself and stating very honestly what you hope to get out of the small group and the meetings. Then go around the circle with each person doing the same, introducing himself/herself and sharing expectations with the rest of the group.

Next, remind everyone of the reason for getting together, the purpose of the small group. Then explain the procedure for your time together, including when you will end and the ground rules for discussion. Also explain that although you are the convener of the group and the discussion leader, you are also a participant and a learner.

If the group has met before, take time for everyone to report on what has transpired in their lives since the last time you got together. If there was an assignment, see how everyone did in carrying it out. If someone won an award, celebrated a birthday, reached a milestone, etc., recognize that achievement. After giving everyone the chance to share, shift the discussion to the topic at hand.

Of course the focus and specific topic of your discussion will be determined to a large extent by the purpose of the group and the material you are covering. If you are studying

KOINONIA

"Koinonia" is the Greek word for in-depth spiritual community. It is what happened in the Upper Room when a bunch of broken people (the "walking wounded") got together, cared for each other, and discovered a whole new power in their lives through the Holy Spirit.

To understand how to get to *koinonia,* think of a baseball diamond with koinonia as home plate. To get to home plate, the group must go around three bases. First base is "history-giving" — sharing your spiritual story with one another. Second base is "affirmation" — responding in the group to each other's story with words of genuine appreciation and thanks. Third base is "goal-setting" or need sharing — where you need to move on in your spiritual life and where you need the support of the group.

From the Introduction to *The Serendipity Bible for Groups,* Lyman Coleman, Editor-in-Chief (Zondervan Publishing Company, 1988), page 13.

the Gospel of Mark together, using the *Life Application Bible Studies,* you will have questions to use in the back of the study guide. If your group is a discussion group of high school friends, formed to discuss important issues, you will already have an issue chosen for that meeting. If this is a small group of student leaders considering the implications of discipleship, undoubtedly you will have a topic to discuss. After the initial time of sharing, start the group on the discussion track for the meeting.

Asking Questions

Regardless of the type of small group, any good discussion will involve asking and answering questions. Although anyone should be allowed to ask questions, it is your responsibility, as the leader, to have good questions to get the discussion started and then keep it going. This means that you should *prepare* for each small group meeting. Don't just show up and depend on the group dynamics and your sparkling personality to carry the day. If there is content to be conveyed, help to be offered, Scripture to be studied, and so forth, you must be prepared.

Preparation begins by thinking through the topic at hand and studying thoroughly any material you have that the group will be using. Preparation also means thinking through the questions you will ask. Even if you are using questions that someone else has written, look them over and adapt them to your group.

Here are some general guidelines for writing and adapting questions:

● **Ask questions that are thoughtful.** Don't use questions that can be answered by yes, no, or another one-word response. That will kill a discussion faster that you can say "anyone else?"

Galatians 6:1 says, "Dear brothers, if a Christian is overcome by some sin, you who are godly should gently and humbly help him back onto the right path, remembering that next time it might be one of you who is in the wrong" (TLB).

In discussing this passage, some leaders might ask: "Should Christians help other Christians?" "Have you ever been helped by another Christian?" "Have you ever done anything wrong?" It may seem obvious that those are poor questions to ask, but Sunday School classes and small groups everywhere are filled with them.

Here's a better set of questions: "What does it mean to be 'overcome by sin'?" "What can a Christian do to help another Christian 'back onto the right path'?" "What are some examples of being 'gentle' and 'humble'?"

I have found that almost all yes or no questions already have a correct answer that the questioner is looking for. So instead of asking the obvious, assume the answer and ask a "why" or a "how" question—force the group to think. Instead of asking, "Should children obey their parents?" ask, "Why do you think God tells children to obey their parents?" or "When is it difficult for you to obey your parents?"

● **Ask questions that are simple, and easy to understand.** If a person has to ask for the question to be repeated, the question is probably too complicated.

If you are discussing teenage loneliness, you might want to ask about the reasons for loneliness. Here's an example of a question that is complex and difficult to understand: "Why, and according to many studies it's true, do you think kids are lonely today, as opposed to my generation when it seemed to be a more carefree era?" The question is complicated because it contains extraneous and confusing phrases. A simple, direct question would be: "Why do you think kids today are lonely?"

Questions can also be complicated by asking too much. For example, you might ask: "Why are kids lonely and what can be done about it?" But that's two questions combined into one. It would be better to discuss the first question first, and then discuss the second one.

● **Ask questions that are interesting.** As you consider each question, put yourself in the shoes of a young person in the group. Would you be interested in answering that question? The best questions almost beg to be discussed.

Sometimes the topic itself is boring because it's not controversial or a felt need. "Pollution," for example, would be a boring topic for young people to discuss because no one is *for* it.

Even very important topics can be boring because kids aren't *feeling* them right now. "Death" is a good example of such a topic. Most kids don't think much about dying, and they live as though they're immortal. (And many of them have never been to a funeral.) Although death is a vital subject to consider and discuss, it may be difficult to get much interaction. But think of how the group would probably talk if someone at school had just died.

With topics that aren't currently relevant or naturally interesting, you will have to work even harder at your questions, perhaps using case studies or real-life illustrations (e.g., from your life, from the news) to set up a moral dilemma, build tension, or create a conflict to be resolved.

RIGHT ANSWERS?

The first thing I've discovered through sad experience is *don't ask a question with a right answer*. The worst offender is one that can be answered with a simple yes or no. I was working with a group of non-Christian high school guys. I wanted to get them thinking about the divinity of Jesus. I was afraid they thought he was merely a good man. After a fun day of skiing we sat down together and I launched out, "What do you think, guys? Is Jesus Christ really God?"

I leaned forward expectantly preparing for a rousing thirty-minute discussion. No one spoke. I'm not sure they even breathed. It was like a prayer meeting — every head bowed; every eye shut. They wouldn't look at me for fear of being called on. I restated the question, "Is Jesus really God?" After the pressure became unbearable, one bold soul took the plunge. "Yes," he said. End of discussion!

From *Getting Together, A Guide for Good Groups* by Dr. Em Griffin (InterVarsity Press, 1982), pages 94–95.

For example, you could describe Gary and Suzanne who had known each other since grade school, but didn't start dating until last year. You could describe how close they had become over the last few months and how they are "in love." Then you could explain that it has been discovered that Gary has cancer, and that the outlook doesn't look good. After telling the story, you could ask the group how Gary and

Suzanne might have felt when they heard the news and how each person might prepare for the possibility of Gary's death. Then you could ask what they would do if they received similar news about someone they loved, or about themselves.

It's even possible to make an interesting subject boring, like dating, a topic near and dear to the hearts of most teenagers. A boring question about dating would be: "What is the purpose of dating?" That sounds like something a teacher or a parent (like me) would ask. Or, "When did dating get started as an American ritual?" Yuck!

Interesting questions on the same subject would include: "What do you hate most about the whole dating thing?" "Describe the ideal date. Where would you go and what would you do?" "Girls: what do you wish guys would change in the way they act on dates?" "Guys: what do you wish girls would change in how they treat you before, during, and after a date?" I'm sure you can see the difference.

Think about your group. Would they want to discuss the questions or would they discuss them simply as a favor to you? Ask questions that are simple, thoughtful, and interesting.

Bring several questions to your meeting, with the questions moving in the direction that you would like the discussion to go. Remember, you are the guide. It doesn't mean that you have to ask all those questions. You may find that after the first question, the group will be off and running. But you will be ready just in case.

Your first question is most important because that will set the tone for the rest of the discussion and because you will usually get to ask that one. This first question, therefore, should be nonthreatening and light, almost like an icebreaker, helping everyone begin to talk and think about the topic. How you react to the answers to this first question is also very important. Be positive and grateful, not disagreeing or correcting.

A good opener for a discussion about the family might be to have everyone describe their favorite family vacation or their favorite television family sitcom. One way to begin talking about fear would be to discuss scary movies that they have seen. An opening question for a discussion of the sovereignty of God could be: "What are some of the more disturbing news stories you've seen on the news or read about lately?"

Next, be ready with a follow-up question or two to get into the topic. In the discussion about the sovereignty of God, for example, you could follow with: "Where is God in all of this bad news? Why doesn't He do something about all the problems in the world?"

Be prepared for the discussion by framing good questions.

Keep it Going

The best way to keep the discussion going, with energy and direction, is to remember your roles as "listener" and "learner" (see chapter 4). As the discussion leader (facilitator), you will be asking questions and encouraging kids to respond and interact. At times, you will also have to act as referee, making sure that one person speaks at a time and reminding everyone of the ground rules. But for the discussion to flourish, remember and heed the following "do's and don'ts."

1. Don't interrupt (unless a person is going way off on a tangent). Remember, you are a listener too. So let each person say what is honestly on his or her heart and mind, even if it's wrong or the opposite of what you think.

2. Don't judge. If you are asking good questions, then often there will not be right or wrong answers. So don't jump on someone who says something off the wall or heretical—let him or her speak. Of course we believe that there is ultimate truth to be discovered and shared. But let the group discover the truth together; don't dish it out to them.

3. Don't make speeches or preach. Even if you know more than the rest of the group put together, your words of wisdom probably will kill discussion and fall on deaf ears. If someone asks for your "expert" advice or your opinion on something, give it calmly, slowly, and concisely. Don't give the impression that you have all the answers and that your way is the only way to think.

4. Do probe and ask for clarification. If someone makes a statement, feel free to ask what he or she meant if you didn't understand or you think it may have been unclear to others. Or you could repeat the person's point in other words: "I hear you saying that you agree with Ted because. . . . Is that right?"

5. Do affirm and encourage. Look for opportunities to compliment individuals for their participation. For example: "That was a good insight, Mary. Thanks for sharing it." "That's good . . . I've never thought of that before." "Yeah, yeah, I can see that. Thanks." This will let everyone know that they can make a valuable contribution to the discussion.

METHODS

Methods that expound mere knowledge are deadly to small groups because they are divorced from the needs of life. Lecture by itself is not an adequate small group method. On the other hand, methods that merely encourage the sharing of life-needs without teaching knowledge will quickly prove irrelevant to pilgrims. And discussion by itself is not an adequate method for small groups either.

Good methods integrate life and truth.

From *Pilgrims in Progress* by Dr. Jim and Carol Plueddemann (Harold Shaw Publishers, 1990), page 52.

---

6. Do try to get everyone involved. If someone is monopolizing the discussion, you could say something like: "Tanya, you've contributed a lot of great thoughts tonight, but there may be some others who haven't spoken up yet who have something to say. Let's give them a chance to speak, and then I'll come back to you, OK?"

If certain kids are quiet, it probably won't help to single

them out by asking them to comment on an issue. Instead, watch for a spark of interest and then fan it. Someone might nod in agreement with something that was said, and you could say: "You look like you agree with that, Len. Do you want to add anything?" And if they do say something, be quick to thank them for their participation. If certain kids never say much, let them know it's all right by catching their eye and giving a quick wink or a smile. You may want to talk with them afterward and explain that whenever they're ready to talk in the group, everyone will be ready to listen.

Handling Obstacles

Even the best discussion leader with the most together group will encounter difficulties from time to time. Here are the most common obstacles and how to deal with them.

● **Apathy** is when an individual or the group greets a question with a yawn. They just don't seem to care. Apathy can be caused by an overpowering leader in the group, an overtalkative person, an irrelevant issue, even mental distraction. If everyone is thinking about Friday's big game, they may find it difficult to discuss the finer points of theology.

Don't confront apathy head-on by saying something like: "Why do we seem so apathetic?" Instead, find the cause and deal with that. Maybe people don't care because the questions are boring or because the discussion has gone off on an irrelevant tangent. If that's the case, stop and bring the discussion back on track.

You may even want to drop the topic and ask: "What do you want to talk about today?" Or you could say, "This topic is boring, let's talk about _____ instead."

If apathy is a reaction to a domineering person in the group, you will have to gently ask that person to back off and to let others speak for a while.

● **Anger** can have the same causes as apathy. There may be personal friction in the group; a topic may have hit a nerve; or someone may have brought his or her anger to the meeting.

When someone reacts sharply, you see fire in someone's

eyes, or you sense that someone is ready to pounce, you could ask the person: "Do you feel angry?" Or you could say, "Jamie, I get the feeling that you don't like what's being said, that you're angry." Then you could ask: "Does anyone else? Why are we feeling this way right now; what's going on?"

If a minor conflict arises between two people in the group, you could try to defuse the situation by making light of it and saying something like: "All right you guys ... we'll settle this once and for all afterward ... a duel at 100 yards ... with lawnmowers." In more intense situations, you may have to speak directly to both parties and ask if they want the group to help referee and arbitrate or if they want to talk about the problem with you after the meeting.

● **Silence.** If everyone is silent, it may be because they are thinking or because they didn't understand the question. Try rephrasing the question. Or you could say something like: "Okay, let's move on to the next question ... " and then repeat the question you just asked.

● **Blocking** is when someone continues to take the opposite and negative position or keeps getting off the subject entirely. Suggest to the "blocker" that the two of you get together afterward to discuss his or her concerns. If a person brings up a totally new topic, especially one that could take the group way off the subject, you could explain that the group could spend hours on that topic, so maybe it would be best held for another time.

● **Hidden agenda.** In some discussions, everything can be going smoothly when suddenly things explode. That's evidence of a "hidden agenda"—somebody's hot button was pushed. You will have to use your good judgment here, but if more than one person reacts, you should probably take time in the group to deal with the issue. You could say something like: "Let's hold the discussion for a while. It seems like there are a lot of feelings bubbling up. How do you really feel right now?" If it's one individual, you should probably deal with that person privately.

Another type of hidden agenda is when someone keeps bringing up a favorite topic, no matter what the rest of the group is talking about. This is another situation best handled individually, after the meeting. At the time, however, a good response would be similar to the one under "Blocking." Ask the person to hold his or her topic for another time.

● **Your feelings.** At times you may find yourself reacting with frustration or anger to what is going on in the group. Someone may verbally attack Christ, Christianity, your church, a relative or something else that you love. You will be tempted to lash out, strike back, and set the record straight. Don't.

At other times you will be tempted to take out your feelings on everyone, giving them a lecture or getting your feelings off your chest. When that happens, explain your feelings to the group. For example, if the discussion isn't going the way you think it should, be honest and say something like: "I have to be honest with you. Right now I'm feeling a little impatient with the way things are going. I wonder if anyone else feels the same way."

In addition to those obstacles, here's what you can say when . . .

● **You suspect that the speaker has no evidence.**
Ask: "Why do you believe that?" or "What have you observed that makes you think that's true?"

● **You feel yourself getting upset and you don't know why.**
Ask: "Does anyone else feel disturbed, confused?" or "Is anyone else uneasy?"

If something bugs you, say so; perhaps others can explain what's going on.

● **When you can't believe what you're hearing.**
Ask: "Do I have your meaning right? Correct me if I don't."
Restating carefully avoids misunderstanding.

● **When an interesting point has been lost in the shuffle.**
Ask: "Could we return to a point that was made earlier?" or "Could we go into this a little more?"

● **When the speaker has lots of examples, but you suspect a way-out conclusion.**
Ask: "I agree with your facts, but what conclusions are you drawing?" This avoids putting words in his or her mouth.

● **When everyone seems too concerned about a detail.**
Ask: "I think I've lost the track. How did we get to this point?" A digression may be leading to an important insight or to nowhere. Find out where it's going.

● **When everyone jumps on a speaker.**
Ask: "Can't we hold those arguments till we've heard him out?"

There's nothing quite like the dynamic give-and-take of an effective small group discussion. In the process of asking and answering questions, thinking things through, listening, and evaluating, people learn. They learn about themselves, how to relate to others, how to dig deeper and really understand an issue, and how to find answers. Take the lead and keep them talking in circles.

UP CLOSE
Introducing the Profiles of Special Small Group Ministries

I am not a snow skier, although I've tried to be from time to time. Skiing looks easy enough when I stand at the bottom of the hill and see skiers of all ages glide effortlessly, around moguls, through powder, and around obstacles, and then suddenly turn and stop. And skiing sounds easy when I stand in the beginners class on the bunny hill and listen intently to the lithe and tan instructor leaning on her poles and demonstrating each move with grace. Skiing still looks easy as I look around and down from the top of the mountain after careening off the chairlift. In one breathtaking view, I see snow, skiers, and the mountain as "one," working in harmony.

But it's a different story when I push off and begin to move down the hill. Suddenly the view becomes quite different as I become personally involved with skiing—out of control and overwhelmed by fear. It's not theory from a distance; it's reality, up close.

Thus far, we have discussed small groups from a theoretical distance, thinking through the rationale, explaining necessary skills and tasks, and outlining possible strategies. Although I've tried to be realistic, after reading the first half of this book, it still is possible for you to have an idealized idea of youth ministry in small groups.

That's why I've included this next section that features profiles of a variety of small group ministries. These are real men and women, working with real kids, putting ministry principles into practice. I call them "profiles" and not "models" because I don't want you to think that I am setting them up as ideal or perfect. Whenever human beings are involved in anything, there will be imperfection—mistakes, tensions, and flaws. So don't think of these ministers as "super-saints" and put them on pedestals. And don't think that by copying them in detail you will be guaranteed success. Glean the best ideas among all of them. Look for the approaches that best fit your particular ministry situation.

The truth is that any ministry plan will take faith, commitment, patience, hard work, and God's power to change lives, and will involve failure as well as success. So instead of trying to copy exactly the ideas and ministry plans of these leaders, emulate their commitment to Christ and to reaching kids, their creativity, and their consistency.

I found that the *philosophies* for the ministries profiled are very similar. They all emphasize the importance of developing strong relationships between the leaders and the group members, building a sense of belonging and community in the group, and communicating biblical content. But the *plans* differ greatly, according to each ministry's specific *purposes*.

In each profile, I try to give you a flavor of the ministry by explaining the need that motivated the leader to use his or her small group approach; that's the "why." Then I present the "what," briefly summarizing the ministry in the following categories: leaders, participants, meetings, and content. I also include the person's address and phone number so that you can contact him or her for more information.

My goal is to give you a better perspective on small group ministry, not from a distance, but a step nearer to reality, up close and personal.

SIX
BREAKING IT DOWN
Discipleship Groups in Barrington, Illinois

n the mid-1970s, the youth group for a suburban Chicago church began to grow. That's not so unusual. But with young, aggressive, talented, and charismatic leaders, a committed core of youth "captains," and an exciting program with music and media, the group grew to huge proportions. The church became a magnet, drawing Christian kids and their friends from the surrounding communities. Soon hundreds of high schoolers were packing out the sanctuary on Tuesday nights.

Eventually the leaders decided to begin a church of their own. They chose an area about fifteen miles to the northwest, where the largest contingent (200+) of kids from the youth ministry lived. These young people along with a smattering of adults and the leaders formed the foundation for Willow Creek Community Church. Tailoring the ministry to people who had been turned off by churches, Willow Creek reached out to hundreds and then thousands of secular suburbanites.

Today, Willow Creek stands as a modern, church growth phenomenon, with a fabulous campus in affluent Barrington, Illinois and 14,000 in attendance each weekend. The youth ministry has kept pace with this growth. Although the philosophy and program have changed over the years, 1,200 kids still attend every Tuesday night. During the course of a year, literally thousands of young people are touched by this ministry.

The Need

Tony Schwartz grew up at Willow Creek, having become a Christian through the youth program during his sophomore year in high school. After graduating from college, Tony joined the Willow Creek staff. For the past eight years, he has been a leader in the youth ministry. Today, Tony is an Associate Director of Student Impact.

Tony thinks the attendance numbers are great, especially when they represent kids finding Christ. But his heart is in *discipleship*, seeing students grow and mature in their spiritual lives. Although Tony and other church leaders were excited with their success in terms of the number of kids being touched by the ministry, a couple of years ago they began to be frustrated with the lack of depth of change occurring in many students' lives.

Tony explains their reactions: "We would see kids come back from college on Christmas or spring break. We'd see them in the mall or on the street and talk to them; and we'd ask, 'Are you walking with the Lord?' They'd look back, and the way they talked, we could tell that nothing was deeply affecting them on a spiritual level. They weren't in love with Christ. That was a major motivator to me personally because there we were in the ministry with tons of people—1,000 kids every Tuesday. All kinds of life and flash. A great band. A lot of dust being created. But at the end of the year, when the dust has settled, it's not a great program that pulls you through; it's who you've got standing next to you that makes the biggest difference. And it's through discipleship that kids grow to the point where they're not in love with anything but the Lord."

That's why Willow Creek decided to move aggressively into small group ministry—to touch kids on a more personal level and to help them grow spiritually.

Up to that point, the church's youth ministry centered around Son City, now called Student Impact, on Tuesday nights (outreach to non-Christians, with about 1,200 in attendance) and Student Insight on Sunday nights (Christian growth for Christians, with about 500 in attendance).

> "At the end of the year, when the dust has settled, it's not a great program that pulls you through; it's who you've got standing next to you that makes the biggest difference."

THE PROBLEM

At first, Tony and the other leaders had difficulty getting kids to become involved in the small groups. In analyzing the situation, they discovered two main reasons for this problem:
- *Busy schedules* — kids were so busy with school, extracurricular activities, dating, work, and so forth that they couldn't afford another night out.
- *Untrained leaders* — because the small group leaders hadn't been trained, the groups weren't very meaningful.

They knew that to make small groups work, those two barriers would have to be removed. In Tony's words, "We had to figure out a way to integrate small groups into a kid's week without killing him, stretching him too far; and we had to figure out a way to train our leaders."

THE SOLUTION

To make small groups a vital part of the ministry and to put them into a realistic time frame, the Student Impact staff developed what they call the "discipleship package" for the Christian kids, uniting Student Insight and small groups in purpose. To make time for small groups, they began alternating the Sunday evening programs. On one Sunday evening, there is Student Insight; on the next, there are small groups.

To improve the leadership training, the leaders come to church at 4 P.M. on small-group Sundays. From 4:00 to 6:00 they are trained and are given the material for their small group meetings *which are still two weeks away*. Then the leaders leave to get their kids and have their meetings.

THE PROCESS

Leaders

The small group leaders are either college-age young people or high school upperclassmen, the top Christian students in the program. Willow Creek's high school ministry is organized around the high schools in the area, and the ministry for each school is led by a Campus Director. Campus Directors include volunteers and some youth ministry interns.

For each grade in the school there are two Grade Level Directors (one guy and one girl), so every school has eight Grade Level Directors. These are volunteer college and high school students (upperclassmen).

The task of the Campus Director is to work with the Grade Level Directors and to lead a small group of students. The Grade Level Director is expected to disciple four or five students (guys or girls) and to build the number of kids involved in Student Impact from his or her grade to 25 (so the total for each school would be 200, 50 from each grade). Each Grade Level Director leads a small group, and during the year, he or she is expected to recruit and train two upperclassmen to be small group leaders.

There are also Team Captains. These are key high school kids who are leaders. Their main responsibility is to be an influence for Christ on their campuses. They also represent and lead their teams at the Student Impact meetings and events. (Usually there is one team per high school, but some teams may have more than one school.) Team Captains may also lead small groups, but it's not required.

The small group leaders come from this leadership pool of Campus Directors, Grade Level Directors, Team Captains, and other upperclassmen, student leaders. Most of these small group leaders are high school students. Presently there are 120 leaders working with 450 kids in small groups.

Participants

At Insight meetings early in the year, kids are challenged to sign up for small groups. Those who sign up are grouped according to the team that they're already on and other personal factors. The Grade Level Directors decide who will go in to which group, with which leader. They try to keep the groups at a maximum of six, including the leader. Groups tend to be made up of kids of the same age and sex (e.g., sophomore girls, freshmen guys).

According to Tony, the ideal participant in a small group is "any Christian who is committed to being consistent." In other words, group members are expected to be active on Sunday and Tuesday nights and to attend all small group meetings.

The goal of this small group plan is to get kids plugged into a four-year cycle. Ideally, a young person would get involved as a freshman or sophomore; then by the junior or senior year, he or she would be leading a group.

At the beginning of the year, when the kids sign up for the small groups, the youth ministry team mails letters to the parents explaining the "discipleship package" and the small group program, and asking for the parents' permission to participate. The parents must give their approval before a young person is allowed to be in a small group.

Meetings

A unique feature of Willow Creek's small group approach is their emphasis on "high involvement." The idea is that each

> "We have to get rid of the four-walls mentality. We've got to put the knowledge and the biblical doctrines in the context of an experience that kids can have together."

small group leader will reinforce the lesson for the week through a group activity. Tony says, "We have to get rid of the four-walls mentality. We've got to put the knowledge and the biblical doctrines in the context of an experience that kids can have together."

So small group leaders are encouraged to look for creative activities that relate to and reinforce their lessons. To teach about vision, one group went to the top of the Sears Tower for their meeting; another group went to a Pearle Vision Center after hours (where one of the mothers worked). To emphasize getting down to business with God, one of the groups met in a conference room in an office building. Another leader put a different twist on the theme and spoke about getting a "tune-up" in their relationship with God. He led this meeting in an auto mechanic's garage. To better understand "endurance," one small group trained for and ran in a 10K race.

Because of the emphasis on creativity and high involvement, the format of the meetings varies from week to week. One session might consist of three principles that arise from a specific Bible passage. Another might involve watching a video of a popular movie and pausing it from time to time for discussion. Or a group might drive to a special location. Tony adds: "We try to solidify certain biblical principles through an experience, a memorable moment."

As mentioned earlier, leaders leave church at 6:00 to pick up the kids between 6:30 and 7:00 P.M. They must get everyone home no later than 9:15. This time limit is strictly enforced because of school the next day.

Content

Tony and others design the lessons and train the leaders. It is hoped that many kids will "graduate" from groups to become group leaders after two years, so the curriculum is on a two-year cycle. These lessons are presented to the leaders two weeks before they are to be taught. Because the groups vary in age, experience, maturity, etc., leaders are given flexibility on their teaching methods and the depth of the teaching.

The main emphasis of the lessons is Bible doctrine, tied to

life: God's will, vision, endurance, prayer, and other similar topics. Bible memorization is also an important part of the lessons. Every participant is expected to bring a Bible, a pen, and his or her journal to each meeting.

Relationships are foundational for Willow Creek's youth ministry, so small group leaders are expected to become involved in their kids' lives. This means contacting group members between meetings: going to a game, going shopping, playing ball, or just talking on the phone. And it means checking up on kids who miss meetings, holding them accountable for their commitments.

"Halftime," a retreat for all the small group members, is held halfway through the school year. Not everyone can come—only those involved in small groups and Insight. The emphasis on the retreat is leadership development, motivating and mobilizing these student leaders for the rest of the year.

Although they've been implementing this ministry for just a short time, Tony is excited about the results and about the future. But the key to these groups according to Tony, is the leader. He tells his potential group leaders: "If you want to take this on, you've got to commit yourself to prayerfully get in so deep with a kid that you live and die with that person. And you have to realize that the most important thing you can impart is your example."

AT A GLANCE
High Involvement Small Groups for
Willow Creek Community Church

Purpose: to give personal attention to kids; to build
  disciples
Type of kids: Christians; usually underclassmen
Leaders: salaried staff, volunteer adults and college stu-
  dents, and selected high school upperclassmen
Size: 4–6 in each group, including the leader
Number of meetings each week: 1 every other week
  (alternating with Insight); groups may do something
  else together between meetings
Length of each meeting: approximately two hours
Unique feature: each meeting features a memorable,
  "high involvement" activity that relates to and rein-
  forces the lesson; most groups are student-led
Content: Bible doctrine, tied to life
Materials: Tony Schwartz is in the process of writing
  the two-year curriculum

To find out more about Willow Creek's high involve-
ment small groups, you can attend:
  Willow Creek Community Church Leadership Conference
  Youth Ministries Track
  Held in October, February, and May of each year
  Call: (708) 382-6200 for more information

SEVEN
DIGGING IN
Bible Study Groups in Seattle, Washington

D enny Rydberg has been a believer in small groups since he began in youth work in the 1960s. One event stands out in his memory: a hiking trip with a group of kids from Washington and Montana, in Glacier National Park. Often along the way they would sit and talk, discussing their lives and the Bible. Through those discussions, the group learned together and grew very close. Denny decided that he would try to replicate that experience when he got back to the city. Since then, his whole life and ministry have tied into small groups. Over the years, Denny also has worked with Bruce Larson and Lyman Coleman. Those pioneers and leaders in the small group movement made a lasting impact on Denny's life and ministry. He believes that "small groups are absolutely necessary to a balanced ministry and to help people grow."

Today Denny works mainly with college groups (University Ministries) through University Presbyterian Church in Seattle, Washington.

> "People need to hear what God is saying. There is also something mysterious about studying the Bible, in that it begins to make a difference in your life. Christians need to be grounded in the Word; they need to spend time in the Word."

THE NEED

The emphasis of Denny's ministry is Bible study. He says: "People need to hear what God is saying. There is also something mysterious about studying the Bible, in that it begins to make a difference in your life. Christians need to be grounded in the Word; they need to spend time in the Word."

When Denny began small group Bible studies, there was no great need or problem that he was trying to address. Instead, he used the small group approach because he thought it made sense. "It just seemed like a good idea that after you had some content, to break people into small groups and have them talk about it with each other."

Denny believes that people learn more through personal interaction with each other and with the Bible text. Although individuals can be helped in a large Bible study, they may be afraid to voice their questions, objections, thoughts, and insights in that setting. A small group, on the other hand, can be much less threatening and intimidating.

Denny also used small groups because he thought that they would be a great place to develop leadership. By giving individuals the chance to lead the Bible studies, they would learn by doing; then they could begin their own small groups and lead others.

Another need met by the small group ministry at University Presbyterian is developing the personal side of the ministry. The church has a large college ministry, with 600-700 students who come out every Tuesday night to a program called "The Inn." During a given week, this program involves over 1,000 students. Small groups help touch individuals who could be lost in the crowd. Denny explains: "We need small groups, not only because it's an excellent way to help people learn and grow, but we need them because folks can get lost in a huge group."

In summarizing why he is involved in small group ministry, Denny says, "There are three reasons that I do small groups: 1. It's a great way to develop community; 2. It's important in our ministry to let people become known to others; 3. It's the best learning style to allow people to interact with the text."

THE PROCESS

Leaders

In Denny's small group Bible studies, the small group leaders are university students who have been trained in the church's "student leadership program." The group leader is the key person for each group; he or she really heads everything up. So the training for these leaders is very important. Group leaders are given a lot of freedom, but Denny and the other full-time staff check with them on a regular basis, on the phone, face-to-face, or in a leaders' meeting. Besides troubleshooting (e.g., Do they need help? Are people showing up?), Denny and his associates try to shepherd the leaders, giving them spiritual food, inspiration, and motivation.

Denny emphasizes that the small group leaders are facilitators rather than teachers. But this involves more than showing up and leading the discussion. The leader is the person who has prepared for the meeting by reading over the material and thinking through the discussion questions. And he or she will share first when everyone "checks in" at the beginning of the meeting. Because these small groups are very informal, the leader of each meeting may vary from week to week, with some groups rotating leadership. But the group leader is responsible for the whole group. He or she will call people who weren't at the meeting, organize group outings, and be alert for personal needs.

Participants

Everyone involved in the college ministry for University Presbyterian Church knows right away that small groups are important. In addition to the groups that meet through the year, there are small groups at camps and conferences and in just about every ministry program. Denny says, "Small groups are just a natural part of being involved in University Ministries, and people know the benefits." So it's not too tough to get kids interested.

At the beginning of the year, the staff advertise for a couple of weeks in a row at the large meetings. Then they have sign-ups. As a result, two hundred get involved right away. During the year, at "The Inn" (the big meeting on Tuesday night), Denny will interview various students about how small groups have impacted their lives. That also helps in recruitment.

> "It's really tough just to throw a group of adolescents in a small group if they don't have some faith and trust in the leaders. I think you have to do more in terms of preparing the way for small groups when you're working with junior high and senior high than you do when you're working with college students."

Denny admits that it might be a bit easier to recruit college students than high schoolers for small groups because of their maturity and their commitment to the ministry. Denny has had extensive experience with adolescents, however, and he explains, "It's real tough to just throw a group of adolescents in a small group if they don't have some faith and trust in the leaders. I think you have to do more in terms of preparing the way for small groups when you're working with junior high and senior high than you do when you're working with college students."

Denny firmly believes that a leader should not try to start a small group with younger adolescents (e.g., 14–17) until that person has built relationships with individual students and they feel comfortable with him or her.

According to Denny, an ideal participant in his small group ministry is someone who shows up every week, is willing to listen, is willing to talk, is willing to reveal a bit of himself or herself to the group, and will work at applying in life what he or she is learning from the Word.

Being a good small group member has nothing to do with how much Bible content a person knows. "In fact," says Denny, "it's great to have in a group those who are new and fresh to the faith because they ask questions that are also new and fresh."

Because these groups are geared to Christians, they are not evangelistic. But non-Christian students have become involved and have come to Christ as a result.

There are a number of factors that determine how kids are grouped, and the approach that is used may change from year to year. Sometimes students choose the groups on the basis of the topic being discussed or Bible book being studied. At other times, the groups are organized around friendships (e.g., fraternity guys, etc.). And sometimes leaders choose their small groups on the basis of when everyone is available; the college schedule can be very hectic. Denny believes that the most effective groups are those with students who already have something in common — "affinity groups."

There are 4–7 kids in each group.

Meetings

The small group schedule for University Ministries parallels the university's quarter system. In other words, a group will meet for eight weeks, during the fall quarter. Then they will decide whether or not they want to stay together for the whole year. So the first quarter is sort of a trial period. With high school students, Denny would also follow the academic year, meeting for a semester, taking time off, then meeting for the rest of the second semester.

Groups meet once a week, with meetings lasting about an hour and a half. And they meet at various places and times, depending on what is convenient for the members.

The typical meeting has three main elements: check-in, Bible study, and prayer, usually in that order.

Check-in begins the meeting with everyone sharing what went on the previous week in their lives. This is not intended to be heavy or deep; they just go around the circle and bring the group up to date. Another way to begin is with a "throw-away question." This is a fun question that gets the ball rolling and helps the group get to know each other better. The leader could ask: "What would you like to be doing five years from now?" "What color or colors symbolize your personality? Explain." "Describe your favorite family vacation." "What living person do you admire most and why?"

The Bible study is *inductive.* That is, they begin with the text and work together to discover the timeless truths and how to apply those truths to their lives today. The group leader uses questions to guide the discussion toward those ends.

Denny believes that there should also be a time of prayer in each small group meeting. The format for this depends on the nature of the group and the decision of the leader. But group members should spend time praying for each other.

Beyond the meetings, the small groups are encouraged to have a service project or to take a trip together. This could be something risky like rock climbing. The main purpose of these activities is to pull the group closer, to develop relationships outside of the weekly meetings.

Members are also encouraged to see at least one other member of the group during the week. There's no "homework" per se (as students, they are already loaded down with assignments), but often there will be accountability points. This is where they hold each other accountable for putting a specific Bible lesson into practice.

Denny explains that affirmation is an important part of the group process. This can't be programmed or planned; but if the group is developing closeness, members will be affirming each other. That's part of what it means to build community. At the end of the year, however, groups are encouraged to close with a strong dose of affirmation, expressing gratitude to each individual as a valued person and member of the group.

Content

The purpose of these small groups is to help believers grow through Bible study, so the Bible is the center of the discussion. A group might do a topical study (e.g., grace, love, relationships, the person of Christ) or a book study. The content focus is left to the leader. Occasionally a group will discuss a book other than the Bible, but that's a rare exception.

The group leaders and the ministry interns write most of the materials used in the small groups. Denny wrote the questions for the *Serendipity New Testament,* so he helps leaders structure the questions that they write for their meetings. Denny believes that writing the Bible studies gives the leaders ownership and helps develop them as creative writers. He adds, "It's also cheaper . . . and it's fun!"

AT A GLANCE
Small Group Bible Studies for
University Presbyterian Church

Purpose: to help believers grow through Bible study and
   to develop community
Types of kids: Christians and seeking non-Christians
Leaders: college students, trained in the student leader-
   ship program
Size: 4–7, plus the leader
Number of meetings each week: one
Length of each meeting: approximately 1½ hours
Unique features: the schedule follows the school sched-
   ule (quarter system); leaders and interns write most
   of the Bible study materials
Content: Bible study—topical study or book study
Materials: most of the materials are written by staff;
   some also use the *Serendipity New Testament*

For more information on the Bible study small groups of
the University Presbyterian Church, contact:

Denny Rydberg
Director of University Ministries
University Presbyterian Church
4540 15th Avenue, N.E.
Seattle, WA 98105
(206) 524-7300, extension 134

EIGHT
REACHING OUT
Evangelistic Small Groups in Cedar Falls, Iowa

hen most of us hear the word "backbone," we probably
envision a part of human anatomy, the spine. Or
thoughts of pain and chiropractors may come to mind.
We may even think of strength and courage. Very few of us
would think of Iowa. Yet, that's where we would find the
"Backbone area," a collection of small towns and farming
communities in the center of the state. The Backbone area
includes Waterloo, Manchester, Edgewood, Colesburg,
Lemont, Strawberry Point, and everything in between.

For many years, Dave Bartlett worked in that region on
the Campus Life staff of Backbone Area Youth for Christ.
Dave's focus was evangelism, reaching non-Christian high
school students with the Gospel of Christ. And so he followed
religiously the Campus Life philosophy and ministry plan,
spending countless hours on campus, building relationships,
holding meetings, sponsoring trips and special events, and
counseling individuals. It was during those years in Campus
Life that Dave began to see the value of small groups as an
effective, evangelistic ministry tool. So about five years ago,
Dave designed and tested his unique brand of small groups.
This approach was so successful that word spread to other

YFC programs. Today it is offered nationally as a YFC ministry model.

Currently, Dave continues to reach kids through small
groups as he ministers in Cedar Falls, Iowa (about 40 miles
from the Backbone area) as the youth director for Orchard
Hill Reformed Church and Nazareth Lutheran Church. Although Dave has left Backbone YFC, the small groups continue to reach young people in that area. Gary Follmann, a
Campus Life staff member, told me that his two schools have
10 groups.

THE NEED

As a dedicated Campus Life staff person, Dave was looking
for a way to reach the most kids, the deepest. Because he
had freedom to try whatever it took to reach that goal, Dave
tried a variety of ministry approaches, including weekly club
meetings, large events, special trips, and other activities.
Having read about LUGs (Living Unit Groups) in the Campus
Life Operations Manual, Dave decided to give small groups a
shot. He continued moving his ministry in that direction
when he discovered that kids were more excited about the
small groups than anything else he had tried. Dave says,
"Seeing their excitement is what caused me to get excited
and realize that this would be a great tool for ministry."

As Dave put his small group ministry together, he analyzed
what kids wanted and needed and decided to meet those
needs. He found that kids were tending to cluster with
friends. They would do everything with a certain group. He
sensed that kids wanted and needed a place to talk, about
anything and everything, with no one judging or grading
them. They wanted to talk things through on their own and
to find answers. He realized that kids needed a place where
they could be totally honest. They wanted to share their real
and deep feelings about issues and about life. These needs
shaped Dave's small group approach.

To meet these needs through small groups, Dave realized
that he would have to break some of the "rules" for LUGs as
outlined in his manual. First, he let the kids put the groups

together, so each one was a group of friends and included a healthy mix of Christians and non-Christians (previously the groups were formed by staff). Second, he allowed, and then encouraged, the groups to be co-ed (previously each group was comprised of either boys or girls, but not both). Third, he focused the groups on discussion and not on content or answers (previously the groups would center around topics or Bible study).

As Dave began his small groups, he didn't abandon his other ministry activities—campus contacting, club meetings, and so forth. But the groups became so successful that he found himself overwhelmed with requests from kids to get involved. In one school, Dave had two outreach clubs and six small groups (he led two of the small groups himself)—all that for a school of 1,000 students.

Dave says that the main goal of these small groups is *to help each young person and the adult leader move closer to God.* This goal is general because each group is spiritually diverse, mixing Christians and non-Christians, each at a different point on the spiritual journey. Through the honest discussions, each person takes a close look at his or her relationship with God, and then takes the next step toward Him.

> "I think Christian growth and discipleship is not so much content based as it is experience and obedience based."

Dave explains it this way: "I think Christian growth and discipleship is not so much content based as it is experience and obedience based. And so if a person is a non-Christian, our goal (to move him closer to God) may mean that he becomes a Christian. Or it may mean that he stops hating God and becomes a seeker. If a kid is a nominal Christian, the goal is that he will gain a better understanding of his relationship with God. If a young person is somewhat committed, hopefully, by going through the same material, he will grow even closer. And this is going on at the same time in the group."

With so many non-Christians involved, the small groups have led to many decisions for Christ.

Another goal of these small groups is to help members learn how to relate to others. This involves learning to listen to each other, to look at each other, to care about each other, and to challenge each other.

These goals are achieved through the group dynamics and the honest discussions much more than through the material being used or topic being discussed.

THE PROCESS

Leaders

As with most small group ministries, the leader plays an important role. He or she is the one who pulls the group together and gets the meeting going. But in Dave's LUGs, the leader is an equal participant with the students in the group, sharing and learning along with everyone else. Dave says, "The most important thing a small group leader can do is be a good listener."

The leader is not a teacher, instructor, or answer-person. He or she brings the sharing activities, but there is no "lesson" to get through, for the lesson comes out of group members' lives and values. The leader also sets the tone of the group as far as depth of honesty and enthusiasm. If the group is not being very honest, usually it's because the leader is not being very honest. That puts a burden on the leader to be real.

Leaders also see group members outside the meetings. Usually this happens naturally because relationships have developed, but leaders are also encouraged to contact kids and to initiate social activities. And often kids will ask to get together one-on-one with the leader to talk in depth about a problem.

The profile for a small group leader is simple: someone who is responsible and is willing to be honest, to be a good listener, and to lead discussions. Dave adds that ministering in this setting is difficult for those who feel like they have to give the answer, "like the parent who listens in order to know which lecture to give," and for those who tend to be judgmental, telling kids when they have done wrong.

When Dave began this ministry, most of his small group leaders were Christian adults, salaried staff, and volunteers. Lately he has found that some students are starting their own small groups. Usually their motivation is to get their friends to talk about God and to share their faith. Dave encourages these student leaders, but he doesn't have a strategy for developing a number of student-led groups.

Dave trains the leaders in how to relate to young people, how to lead discussions, and group dynamics. But even with careful screening and training, about half of the leaders do not continue after their first small group. Some feel uncomfortable with young people and would rather minister with adults. Others find it difficult to be so honest. And there are those who just don't fit in for a variety of reasons.

Participants

LUGs begin with a staff person like Dave talking with a Christian student or two about these small groups, their purpose and philosophy. If these students are interested, Dave asks them to think of a group of friends that they could invite to an initial meeting. It's important that these kids be friends and that the high school groups include both boys and girls. Dave has found that high schoolers tend to be MORE honest when both sexes are included. But he doesn't recommend co-ed groups with junior high kids; there the opposite sex will be a distraction. Dave also keeps the groups at 6–10 members, including the leader.

At that introductory meeting, the leader explains the purpose of the group: to get to know each other better and to talk honestly about important issues that concern them. The leader also goes over the rules:
1. Be honest or be silent.
2. Have total confidentiality.
3. Keep the commitment to attend the meetings.

Then they have a discussion that helps break the ice and that gives them a flavor of future meetings.

At the end of the meeting, they are asked if they want to meet again next week. That's when the leader asks for a longer commitment, like meeting for five more weeks. Then the group is closed; that is, no one else can join the group during the next five weeks.

Eventually, recruitment is not a problem because kids hear about the groups from their friends and want to get in. Dave now has a waiting list for future groups. He explains: "We have kind of a rolling list. In fact, we carry this list in our Daytimers, the kids who have shown interest. Then, when we're ready to start a new group with a Christian student, we show him the list of those who said they were interested."

Dave says that there really isn't an "ideal" participant; he's found that all kinds of kids get involved. Often the groups attract young people who have dropped out of the normal youth program. Dave believes that one reason they drop out is that traditional youth ministries tend to act as though school is the center of their lives. In reality, their jobs, their friends, and their lifestyles are most important to them. Dave adds, "To build a youth program aimed at a student of a high school is probably ten to fifteen years behind where most juniors and seniors in high school are. So if someone is trying to reach and challenge kids who have dropped out, he should try this ministry approach."

Dave has also found that kids from affluent families love these small groups. They have done everything from flying to Hawaii for vacation to going to a Superbowl, but they've nev-

---

"To build a youth program aimed at a student of a high school is probably ten to fifteen years behind where most juniors and seniors in high school are. So if someone is tring to reach and challenge kids who have dropped out, he should try this ministry approach."

er really TALKED IN DEPTH with anyone. The small groups give them a chance to participate instead of being vicarious observers.

Meetings

Groups meet at anytime throughout the week. Some are late at night, after kids get off work. Some are held after supper; some in the mornings. Dave encourages youth workers to have one group just before and one just after their church youth group meeting. That way both the leader and the kids won't have to have another night out.

The structure for the meetings depends on the leader and how the group is progressing. He or she is given a proposed schedule and curriculum (discussion questions and activities) for each meeting. In this curriculum, there might be five different activities for one hour. More important than the suggested activities is what is happening in the group. The leader can throw out the schedule at any time. Dave explains, "What's important is their lives, their reality. So any time the curriculum is not helping the leader get there, he can throw it out and come up with something different, right on the spot. But the purpose of the curriculum is that very thing — to surface where we are. What happened this week? Where are our heads and hearts?"

Trust and honesty are vital for the success of these groups. So participants are told that there are three levels of honesty: honest, more honest, and most honest. "Honest is when you don't want to lie, so you tell your friend what he asks. More

> "Honest is when you don't want to lie, so you tell your friend what he asks. More honest is deeper, when you share what you're feeling and who you are. Most honest is that level that very few of us ever get to, even with ourselves. 'This is how I'm really feeling inside. This is it. This is the bottom of who I am.' "

honest is deeper, when you share what you're feeling and who you are. Most honest is that level that very few of us ever get to, even with ourselves. 'This is how I'm really feeling inside. This is it. This is the bottom of who I am.' "

The meetings are designed to last an hour, and at most, 75 minutes.

Content

Because there was nothing written for this small group ministry approach, Dave put together his own materials, pulling from various sources including Campus Life Resource Manuals, the Ungame, and others. Eventually, Dave wrote a manual entitled *Honest to God* which is sold and distributed by Youth for Christ/USA. This manual contains curriculum for 16 meetings. As you would expect, it is packed with discussion starters, questions, and activities that help members honestly express their ideas and feelings. The emphasis in the first few meetings is communication, using these topics: Introductions, More Introductions, Communicating with Words, Nonverbal Communication, and Compliments. The other topics include: Facing Life's Tensions, Important Values, Observations on Life, Honesty, People Differences, Self-Esteem, Priorities, Goals, Friendship, Family, and Finale.

Dave has also authored *Honest to God II* and a training booklet entitled *Changing Lives.*

Although the schedule will vary from week to week and from group to group, a typical meeting would include a brief introduction to the topic (5 minutes), an opening activity or discussion starter (15 minutes), discussion (15 minutes), another activity (15 minutes), and the leader sharing how the Bible relates (10 minutes).

As mentioned earlier, the curriculum has weekly objectives that tend to be more relational than educational. In other words, the success of a specific meeting is determined more by how the members related to each other and interacted with the subject than any specific lesson they learned.

Dave recognizes that this approach will be frustrating to many youth leaders, especially those who tend to be straight-line thinkers. And many may reject this model because they can't imagine that anything spiritual would be accomplished in the meetings. But Dave reports that more kids have come to Christ through these groups than by any other method he's used or seen. He says, "These groups work because they're honest and very affirming. And they work because kids have a great desire for intimacy and a great desire to take risks. They find intimacy in these groups, and they find answers—from their friends, from the leader, and from the Bible."

AT A GLANCE
Evangelistic Small Groups
in Cedar Falls, Iowa

Purpose: to help bring kids and the leader closer to God

Types of kids: any young person who wants to get involved, usually friends of Christian kids in the youth group

Leaders: professional staff, adult volunteers, some upperclassmen, Christian students

Size: 6–10, including the leader

Number of meetings each week: one

Length of each meeting: 60-75 minutes

Unique features: kids put together the groups (their friends); high school groups are co-ed by design; curriculum centers around discussion and experience rather than content

Materials: *Honest to God, Honest to God II,* and *Changing Lives* written by Dave Bartlett, and other materials that the leaders write for their groups

For more information on evangelistic small groups, contact:

Dave Bartlett
Youth Director, Orchard Hill Reformed Church
and Nazareth Lutheran Chuch
1504 W. 5th Street
Cedar Falls, IA 50613
(319) 266-9796 or (319) 277-5561

nine
GIVING SUPPORT
Small Groups for Teenage Mothers in Waukegan, Illinois

tretching north of Chicago and the close suburbs, Lake County, Illinois encompasses many small towns and lakes all the way to the Wisconsin border. With numerous farms and fields, it would be easy to picture this as strictly a rural area or a peaceful vacation spot for city dwellers; or, seeing the large homes along the tollway, as a preferred location for executives' mansions. But Lake County also has cities — not huge, but complete, with factories, ethnic neighborhoods, and a mix of races and economies, and the Great Lakes Naval Training Center. In fact, some of the most needy areas in Illinois are there, in Waukegan, North Chicago, and Zion.

For decades, Youth for Christ has ministered in Lake County, through Campus Life clubs, Youth Guidance, and other programs. A few years ago, however, staff members tried a new approach. Aware of the severe problem of teen pregnancy, Carla Waterman began "Teen Moms," a small group ministry for young, and usually unmarried, mothers. When Carla began this ministry, there was nothing like it in the area. Eventually the Lake County Health Department began a program for girls in school who became pregnant, teaching them about pregnancy, their options, and what to expect. But they offered little or nothing for those who delivered and kept their babies.

In 1988, Jim and Donna Speer moved to Lake County. Jim came to teach at Trinity Evangelical Divinity School (Deerfield, Ill.), and Donna looked for a ministry of her own. Having served inner city churches in New York and Chicago, the Speers were committed to urban ministry. So hearing about Teen Moms, Donna got involved. She wasn't motivated so much by the fact that it was a small group ministry, but by the needs of the girls, most of whom came from disadvantaged homes. Today, Donna heads this ministry to about 40 girls a year in Waukegan.

THE NEED

There is a great need for a ministry like Teen Moms. When young, unmarried girls get pregnant, they are often alone, rejected by the babies' fathers, their friends, and often their families. They are usually poor and often come from single parent families with no fathers. Donna tells of a 12-year-old mom in the group, "She's still a kid—she's not even a teenager! These kids need acceptance, love, and practical help with their babies."

> "It goes back to the need for male acceptance. That's why their mothers became pregnant. Usually there are no male role models; there are no men in the home who love them. And that's all they're looking for, just acceptance. That's a normal human need!"

These girls almost always keep their babies, perhaps thinking that because their mothers did it, they can do it too. Donna says, "It goes back to the need for male acceptance. That's why their mothers became pregnant. Usually there are no male role models; there are no men in the home who love them. And that's all they're looking for, just acceptance. That's a normal human need!" Through Teen Moms, they can find acceptance, love, and practical help.

The goal of Teen Moms is to teach these girls parenting skills, to lead them to Christ, and to help them understand what it means to be a Christian on a day-to-day basis.

THE PROCESS

Leaders

There are two levels of leadership for Teen Moms. First, there are the group leaders which include Donna and adult volunteers. Second, there are "mentor moms." These are volunteers who care for individual girls in the group. All the leaders are women.

The main tasks of the group leaders are to bring girls to the group meetings, to lead the meetings, and to teach the life skills and other lessons. Group leaders also plan the weekly meetings. With more than one leader per group, they operate as a team, planning each meeting together and taking turns running the meetings.

The role of the mentor moms is to provide personal support and counsel. A mentor mom might take her girl shopping or to church or bring her home to bake cookies. Donna says: "One of the girls called me and said, 'I have a final exam at school and don't have anyone to watch my baby. She's got bronchitis. Is there anybody who can come and watch her?' Well, at that time, one of the girls was living in my home, so I said, 'How about Liz? She just sits at home.' So I brought Liz over to her house."

The leaders for Teen Moms are a special breed. Donna explains: "I would want to make sure that they were called by God to do this, that this was something God had given them the faith to do, because there are a lot of people who are well-meaning but have no real clue as to what they are getting into." When interviewing a potential leader, Donna tries to give her a realistic idea of what to expect.

Training for the leaders is very important because of the

special needs of the girls and their difficult backgrounds (e.g., poverty, single-parent families, etc.) Sometimes it takes years to overcome the middle-class, white orientation and to appreciate and understand the needs of the low-income, black community. Leaders need the extensive training of a missionary going to a cross-cultural situation. The young mothers may live just a few minutes away from those women, but, in many ways, they are worlds apart.

Another emphasis of Donna's training for the leaders is that group members are just kids. The temptation is for leaders to think of the girls as "mothers" and "parents," and then to project their own idea of "mother" and "parent" onto them. In reality, they're young and immature. Leaders are encouraged to let the girls enjoy their childhood as much as possible, letting them be silly and play games, but also teaching them discipline, budgeting, and other life skills.

Donna also teaches her leaders that by working with the girls and their families, they are linked to a whole world. She says, "Their families know so many people! When you are driving around town, they point out So-and-so down the street, and So-and-so across the street. They go to the store, and they know two or three people there. Their networks are just amazing; so when we minister to a family, things happen! Whole families have been ministered to as a result of our working with one girl."

"Their networks are just amazing; so when we minister to a family, things happen! Whole families have been ministered to as a result of our working with one girl."

All the leaders are encouraged to visit the girls during the week, between meetings, and to be available to help the girls when they need special help. But they should not be seen as somebody whom the girls can call anytime they need a ride to the grocery store, because one of the goals of the program is to help these girls fend for themselves and not always be dependent on charity or hand-outs. There are general guidelines for what mentor moms and group leaders should and should not do.

Participants

The program of the Lake County Health Department includes a class in school for pregnant girls. In this class, girls learn how to take care of themselves during pregnancy, what delivery will be like, and so forth. At some point in the semester, the Teen Moms staff is invited to come into the class to explain the program. That's how many girls hear about Teen Moms.

But Donna is quick to point out that she is no longer recruiting: "I have simply too many girls, and at this point we are just responding to the friends of the girls. Most of the girls learn about the program through word of mouth."

Donna interviews each interested girl, letting her know what the group is about. She emphasizes that Teen Moms is a Christian organization and that they present biblical principles as a framework for living. Donna says, "I haven't found much opposition to our Christian emphasis. People screen themselves. If they aren't interested in hearing that, they don't come." Donna takes almost everyone who wants to join, except those who are over 21 or who will turn 21 during the school year.

Group members are asked to become involved for at least a year, but this is not a hard and fast commitment. If a girl misses a number of meetings, she is asked whether or not she is still interested. Donna finds that they don't often have someone who comes a few times and then drops out.

There really is no "ideal" participant, and those who need the program the most often require the most effort from the leaders. Some moms' phones are disconnected every other week; some find themselves homeless; and some are abused by their mothers' current boyfriends. There is a direct correlation between how much support the girls get at home and how many needs they have. This ministry involves loads of intensive care. Donna says, "I have one of the girls and her baby living in my home. She's 18 and homeless. Hopefully she'll be getting an apartment soon."

There is quite a lot of contact among the girls between meetings, especially for those who are still in school. And the older ones are encouraged to get together and share child care. Many of the girls who have "graduated" from the group still meet together for Bible study. Others have become involved in various churches.

Meetings

The Teen Moms groups meet once a week, usually on Monday nights from 6:00 to 7:30. Attendance for each group ranges between 10 and 15. There is a different mix of girls each week, however, because of sick babies, bad weather, homework, or other problems that come up. All the girls and their babies are picked up by the group leaders. Child care is provided for three groups: infants, toddlers, and older children. This is staffed by volunteer, child care workers.

The meetings last an hour (from 6:00 to 7:00). Then, the girls go get their babies and they all get together for refreshments. This provides an important time of interaction.

Each meeting is divided into four parts. First, there are opening games (about 10 minutes) to help loosen up the group and give them the chance to have fun together. Donna says that they love to play "Win, Lose, or Draw." The second part is the lesson for the evening. This takes anywhere from 30 to 45 minutes. Next there is a devotional talk by one of the leaders. This usually involves taking a verse and seeing how it applies to what they've just discussed. The meeting concludes with prayer requests and praying for each other.

In addition to the weekly meetings, every fourth week there is a special event or activity, like going bowling, having a party, or learning a craft. These events provide opportunities for fun and for building relationships.

Content

The purpose of the small groups is to meet the needs that these girls have; therefore much of the content centers around teaching parenting skills and life skills. But another major focus is spiritual development, presenting the girls with the message of Christ and showing them how Christ can change their lives. So the Christian message is woven throughout each meeting.

The parenting skills include all the aspects of parenting, anything having to do with the child or raising a child— bonding with the child, reading to the child, bathing the child, proper hygiene, and so forth.

The life skills area deals with the other aspects of their lives. The girls must see that having and raising this baby is not *everything* in life. They must think of what they will do next, how they will get their education or GED, their long-term goals, etc.

Spiritual development involves their relationships with God. Topics here include prayer, women of faith in the Bible, discipleship, growing as a Christian, and others.

Sometimes the meetings include homework. This could mean having the girls write down what they do every day, or what they eat every day. Or it could involve memory verses. The assignments vary greatly depending on the needs and the lessons.

Donna is always looking for curriculum that will work in these groups, and she has contacted churches, black ministries, and others. So far, however, she hasn't found much, and so she and the other leaders write their own. Donna would love to talk with anyone who has good programming materials for inner city youth.

Donna adds, "Although these girls have tremendous needs, their lives can change, through love, education, and most of all, the power of the Holy Spirit. And that's what Teen Moms is all about."

AT A GLANCE
Small Groups for Teenage Mothers
in Waukegan, Illinois

Purpose: to teach teenage mothers parenting skills and life skills, to lead them to Christ, and to teach them the basics of the Christian life

Types of kids: any interested teenage mother under the age of 21

Leaders: professional staff and adult, women volunteers

Size: 10–15, plus the leaders

Number of meetings each week: one

Length of each meeting: 60 minutes, followed by 30 minutes of refreshments and conversation

Unique features: all of the participants are young, unmarried girls with babies

Materials: Donna has written her own curriculum

For more information on Teen Moms, contact:

Donna Speer
Director of Teen Moms
Lake County YFC
2835 Belvedere, Suite 104
Waukegan, IL 60085
(708) 244-4050

TEN
GOING DEEPER
Spiritual Growth Small Groups in Knoxville, Tennessee

Gwyn Baker qualifies as a youth work "veteran," having ministered to high school and junior high students for nearly twenty years. For half of that time, she and her husband directed a camp. Presently, Gwyn serves as Director of Family Ministries at the Lake Forest Presbyterian Church in Knoxville, Tennessee.

Gwyn's interest in small groups was sparked by her own positive experiences as a member of various groups at camps and conferences. In fact, Gwyn says that eventually she would leave a conference feeling cheated if she hadn't had time to process in small groups what she had heard in the general sessions.

Also, in the early years of Gwyn's ministry, she went through Lyman Coleman's Serendipity training where she learned the theory behind small groups. That sold her on this ministry approach. This was confirmed during her years at the camp when Gwyn saw how kids benefited from being in small groups. "Campers came from all over. Putting kids in small groups helped them see right away that they were with people who cared."

Today, Gwyn uses small groups in every aspect of her

ministry—ongoing groups with junior highers or senior highers, one-time groups for Sunday School classes, youth meetings, or retreats, and special groups for mission trips. The basic purpose of all her small groups is spiritual growth; in Gwyn's words, "to make kids independent of the world and dependent on Christ, and to make them thinkers."

THE NEED

As she began her ministry at Lake Forest Presbyterian, Gwyn used small groups out of necessity, almost as crowd control. She says, "I had mainly junior high boys when I came to this church. And it was nearly impossible to do a lesson or get anything accomplished because of their energy and the intense picking on each other. I divided the youth group into groups of three, each with an adult leader. Their purpose was to discover what they could about the lesson. It made such a difference! We did it for survival! In reality, it was 'divide and conquer.' That may not sound very spiritual, but the kids weren't getting anything when they were controlling the group themselves."

> "I divided the youth group into groups of three, each with an adult leader. Their purpose was to discover what they could about the lesson. It made such a difference! We did it for survival! In reality, it was 'divide and conquer.' That may not sound very spiritual, but the kids weren't getting anything when they were controlling the group themselves."

In Gwyn's experience, small groups are especially helpful with kids who have been raised in the church. When their parents make them attend every week, these young people tend to leave God at church on Sunday. Gwyn says, "Small groups make God relevant to what's going on in their lives. When I meet a group of kids for lunch, away from the church and in their world, and we talk about dating life, I can use their real-life examples to make God real!"

Gwyn is committed to building relationships and meeting individual needs, but she finds that difficult to do in a crowd where there are so many people and where communication is difficult. In small groups, however, she and the other adult leaders can truly listen to kids and minister to them individually, pointing them to Christ.

THE PROCESS

Leaders
Besides Gwyn, the leaders for the small groups are adults in the church who have expressed an interest or who have been recruited by Gwyn to serve. The main qualifications are spiritual maturity, willingness to learn, and the ability to build relationships with kids. Gwyn spends time training these leaders in ministry skills, and they meet weekly before the youth come to Sunday night youth group to go over the content for their small group meetings.

The leaders for these small groups are to be helpers or guides, not teachers. They are responsible for bringing content to the meeting and leading the discussions, but their main task is to listen. Gwyn describes the leader as, "the person who pulls each person out, as it says in Proverbs, 'Someone draws deep water forth.' The leader sets the tone and helps group members share what they are feeling inside."

It is also important for each leader to serve as a "protector." In other words, he or she protects members from putdowns and criticisms from others in the group. This begins by explaining the "no knock" policy, and then enforcing it. This policy is important because kids need to feel that they can say what they really believe and feel and not be judged. Gwyn explains, "Right or wrong, kids need a place where they can express themselves and be who they really are."

Gwyn's goals with her leaders are to get them to feel confident about their skills and to teach them how to prepare for each small group meeting. But when they're in the meetings, they should be able to "let go" and let the group set the agenda. She says, "I think it's very important for them to be able to shift, to flex, to listen, and to move the way the group needs to go. They can't be rigid, but they should provide a structure."

Also Gwyn encourages her leaders to look for fringe kids, those who aren't fully involved in the youth group, and build relationships with them. Hopefully, then, those kids will want to join a small group.

PARTICIPANTS

Young people get into the small groups in a variety of ways. At times Gwyn will handpick certain kids to be on a "leadership team to help in the children's ministry. Members of this group develop leadership skills through planning their meetings and "on the job" evaluations.

Some of the small groups have organized on their own. Gwyn explains: "In my senior high group, kids created a discipleship group themselves. They meet on Friday mornings before school. We give them support, ideas, and guidance, but we want it to be their group."

But most of the small groups arise out of a *need* and aren't preplanned or intentional. For example, following a retreat, several kids responded to the speaker's messages on self-image, so Gwyn started a small group with them.

Usually, Gwyn offers small groups at the beginning of the school year, and those who are interested sign up. Others she hand picks because of needs she sees.

The membership of these groups isn't rigid; changes can be made. But once the dust settles, kids are expected to stay in their groups for the term. The groups range in size from 4–8, including the leader.

High school groups can include both sexes and a variety of ages, interests, and personalities. With junior highers, however, Gwyn goes more slowly, placing kids into groups as the year progresses. She also recommends dividing junior highers by sexes. Gwyn also uses small groups at every meeting, assigning everyone to small groups for discussion.

The ideal member of one of Gwyn's groups is someone who makes the group a priority. This person would attend all group meetings, take the time to prepare for the meetings, and invest himself or herself in the group.

MEETINGS

Kids are asked to make a short-term commitment to the group, usually for about six weeks. When the groups go longer, Gwyn finds that the enthusiasm wanes. After six weeks, the groups take time off. Then they are reorganized and begin again for another six weeks.

Each meeting is about an hour and a half long, and has three main divisions. First there's the "warm-up." This gives kids the chance to have fun together and to make the transition into the study. Leaders use discussion starters or simple games for the warm-ups.

Next, the group moves into the lesson for the meeting. This can be a discussion of an important topic or a study of a book of the Bible. Gwyn has taught her leaders to start where their kids are, so that means asking questions. For example, if the Bible chapter is on fear, the leaders may want to help kids discuss the fears in their lives first, before digging into the Bible. This would set the stage for discovering the Bible truths and applying them to life.

The final part of each meeting is devoted to prayer. Often the leader will divide the group into twos, giving them time to share their needs with each other and to pray for each other. Kids change prayer partners each week so that they get to know everyone in the group.

Sometimes the groups have assignments, especially when they are studying a specific Bible book. Members are expected to be prepared for the next meeting.

CONTENT

Because the purpose of these small groups is to help kids grow spiritually, the content is strongly biblical. Usually groups center their studies around a Bible book, but from time to time they use other resources. One of the goals is to help kids learn to study the Bible on their own, so they are taught how to use a concordance, a Bible dictionary, and other study tools.

> "Several times I've said to the girls, 'Don't take my word for it. Dig in the Bible and find out for yourselves.' I want to build confidence in them, so they don't have to depend on someone else . . . they can find the answers themselves."

Gwyn says, "We're talking about sexuality now, and several times I've said to the girls, 'Don't take my word for it. Dig in the Bible and find out for yourselves.' I want to build confidence in them, so they don't have to depend on someone else . . . they can find the answers themselves."

Gwyn has written her own materials, but she has also used a variety of resources including those from Serendipity, David C. Cook, and Victor Books.

Gwyn uses small groups because she wants to see kids grow in their faith, and she believes this is the best way to accomplish that goal.

AT A GLANCE
Spiritual Growth Small Groups
in Knoxville, Tennessee

Purpose: to help kids become independent of the world
and dependent on Christ
Types of kids: Christian young people from the church
youth ministry (both junior high and senior high)
Leaders: adult volunteers
Size: 4–8, including the leader
Number of meetings each week: one, but kids may be
put in different groups during their youth group on
Sunday evenings
Length of each meeting: 1½ hours
Unique features: all youth group members are assigned
to small groups; Gwyn selects certain kids for special
leadership groups
Materials: Serendipity materials, *Pacesetters* and *Hot
Topics* from David C. Cook, Small Group Studies by
Richard Dunn, from Victor Books, and others; Gwyn
also writes some of the studies

For more information on spiritual growth small
groups, contact:

Gwyn Baker
Director of Family Ministries
Lake Forest Presbyterian Church
714 Lake Forest Drive
Knoxville, TN 37920
(615) 577-2800

ELEVEN
BUILDING COMMUNITY
Small Groups for Urban Youth in Chicago, Illinois

America's great cities are vibrant, exciting, and teeming with life. Well-dressed and confident executives fill skyscraping offices where they buy, sell, and make earthshaking decisions; brightly lit storefronts beckon to passers-by to enter and spend; scores of four-star ethnic restaurants provide delectable fare; world-class artists, entertainers, and athletes perform for adoring fans; parades, festivals, and parties pack the city's social calendar.

That's one view of urban life.

But beneath the glitter and show there's another. It's the city of ghettos, corruption, gangs, abuse, public aid, crime, drugs, and neglect . . . of broken streets and broken lives . . . of dead ends and continuing cycles of poverty and violence. This picture isn't nearly so pretty, but it's real. The truth is that our mega-cities are filled with countless men, women, and children, pressed together and struggling to live.

Nowhere is youth ministry more needed than in the city. If for no other reason, the numbers should draw us there — that's where the kids are. But in light of the staggering needs and the limited resources, many youth leaders feel "led" to "greener pastures."

Russ Knight is an exception. For nearly three decades, he has given his life for young people in the city. As a student volunteer, as a YFC staff member, and now as a ministry consultant working with a number of churches, Russ has shared Christ with thousands of kids in Chicago's neighborhoods and schools. In the process, he has developed an effective ministry model. Russ uses this model in his own ministry, and he gives it away to churches in the city.

THE NEED

As Russ analyzed his work a number of years ago, he began to realize that although the ministry was successful in terms of numbers and programs, there did not seem to be much success in individual lives. Kids would come to large meetings and events where they would be challenged to live for Christ, but then they would receive very little guidance about how to put their faith into practice. He saw kids with tremendous potential but also with tremendous barriers to reaching that potential. Broken families, poverty, gang activity, and other pressures made it difficult for young people to grow and mature in their faith.

To Russ the answer was obvious: personal involvement with individuals, taking time to listen, counsel, and teach. But Russ also knew that he could never see all those kids, build all those relationships, and meet all those needs by himself. And he knew that the ministry could never afford the necessary army of full-time workers to do the job. So Russ designed the "Take 5" plan.

In short, Take 5 is a small group ministry model designed for urban churches. It is volunteer oriented and relationship intensive. Each Take 5 group includes an adult, Christian couple working with just five kids, creating a small group of seven. The purpose of each small group is to build community, close and caring relationships, thus demonstrating what the church should be and could be. Adult leaders, are to be counselors, friends, teachers, and models of the Christian life. In a Take 5 group, a young person receives acceptance, love, guidance, friendship, support, and instruction.

THE PROCESS

Leaders

The leaders of the small groups are usually married couples. Each couple, called "coaches," works with five kids, the "team." It's important that the team be co-ed. The reason for using married couples and for having both sexes in each group is that one of the main tasks of the coaches is to provide a positive and healthy example of a Christian couple. Russ explains: "A lot of urban kids are without good models of love, family, and so forth, so Christian couples become models and even surrogate parents."

> "A lot of urban kids are without good models of love, family, and so forth, so Christian couples become models and even surrogate parents."

The idea is that the coaches will be able to transfer values by demonstrating love, commitment, and Christian living. Russ adds, "They teach informally as well as formally, so there's a lot of 'catching' going on, rather than just talking about what a family ought to be or how a husband and wife should treat each other, and so forth."

Including both sexes in a group also helps teach what the Church should be like, as diverse types of people learn to get along, respect each other, and work together.

Single adults may be leaders, with this adjustment: men work with guys and women work with girls. In these situations, guy and girl teams are brought together for some of the activities and lessons.

The most important qualifications for group leaders, then, is that they are adults who are strong in their faith and who are good role models. No special knowledge or training in Bible or theology is required because the weekly programs are highly structured and volunteer-friendly (more on this later).

Russ spends time training his leaders and encouraging them during the year, helping coaches understand the group process, going over the materials, and troubleshooting.

For the most part, leaders are recruited from a specific church to work with kids in that church whom they already know. More experienced leaders are given kids from the neighborhood, or assigned kids that they don't know very well if at all. Russ also has a couple of school teachers as Take 5 coaches, working with students in their school.

Because five is a small, manageable number to work with and because materials, training, and support are provided, Russ has had little trouble finding good leaders. He explains: "For years these men and women have wanted to help, to make a difference in the community for Christ. This gives them the chance."

"Often the people we recruit have turned down being Sunday School teachers because they didn't think they had time to do it. When they see what we're doing and especially that they have only five kids to work with, they tend to say, 'Oh well, that's different! I can do that!' "

On invitation, Russ and his staff will hold a workshop in a church to explain the Take 5 plan and to recruit leaders. He adds, "Often the people we recruit have turned down being Sunday School teachers because they didn't think they had time to do it. When they see what we're doing and especially that they have only five kids to work with, they tend to say, 'Oh well, that's different! I can do that!' "

The coaches main tasks are: to pull the group together relationally and socially, to lead the small group meetings, and to be in touch with group members between meetings and activities, building individual relationships.

Russ believes that it is important to enlist the support of parents, and he finds that most are very happy to have someone else interested in their kids and in spending time with them. Currently, Russ is working on ways to help parents work with their own kids.

With his leaders, Russ emphasizes that who they ARE is much more important than what they know. He states: "We are the agenda. We are the ministry. And so I constantly remind our leaders that they always have to be looking at themselves—there's nothing more imporant than them being there. There's nothing more important than them being who they say they are—having integrity and showing kids what it means to be conformed to the image of Christ."

Participants

Kids can become involved in Take 5 in a number of ways. In some instances they may also be involved in a church youth group and have been selected to become part of Take 5. In other churches, kids are given the opportunity to sign up for the program. Churches who have community and neighborhood ministries for kids off the street use Take 5 with young people who are relatively new to the church.

In many situations, leaders choose their group, usually kids they already know. In small churches, for example, this might be the whole youth group! Experienced leaders may be assigned to fringe kids or to those that they have never met.

There are times that groups are put together for specific reasons. Russ explains: "We may decide that we want to spend time working on a particular issue with five kids who are all seniors—this is our last shot at them. Or we may have groups of all freshmen—we want to begin on the ground floor with them and try to keep the group together for four years. Or there may be a group of kids who just came to the church and are new Christians."

In some cases, Take 5 groups stay together for years. In others, groups are reshuffled each year.

Groups are put together according to the needs of kids and the types of leaders available. In some situations, the coaches are recruited first; they are prepared to take groups as they develop. At other times, however, there is a waiting list of kids who want to get in.

There is no profile of the ideal participant. Any young person who wants to get involved is welcome. It is important to remember that in most of the participating churches, Take 5 is *in addition to* their regular youth program. In some, it is a *restructuring of* the whole youth ministry.

Meetings and Content

As mentioned above, the program is highly structured, with groups meeting once a week throughout the year. Meetings may be held on any day of the week that is convenient for everyone in the group, but most of the groups meet on weekday evenings. The Take 5 program is designed around a monthly format based on four weeks in a month.

WEEK 1 During the first week, the group goes bowling together. The purpose of this is to help group members get to know each other better and to help coaches know each young person personally. Bowling is a great sport for this because of the many opportunities to talk during the waiting time while other kids are bowling. And in this sport the adult coaches are seen as regular people and not "older leaders" as they roll the ball down the lane.

Bowling also works well because it's the kind of activity that urban youth can afford. And leaders can pick up the entire group in a station wagon and take off for the alley— they don't have to hire a bus to take the whole youth group. Bowling is cheap and convenient.

WEEK 2 This is the week for Bible study or "rap time," depending on where the group is. Kids off the street wouldn't be used to Bible study and would be uncomfortable in a formal setting; they would be more used to rap time, casually talking about anything and everything. In rap time, the leader is a discussion facilitator, asking questions and bringing up topics that kids are interested in.

Kids from churches and those who are more advanced can jump right into Bible study. Most of the groups use the book of Romans. Others might study another book, a special topic, or the whole Bible in general. The format is discussion rather than lecture, and coaches are encouraged to ask questions instead of giving answers and to help each individual feel like he or she is making a contribution.

The purpose of rap time is to help kids talk things through, learn from each other, and find answers. The purpose of the Bible study is to help them learn their way around the Bible and to discover and apply biblical truths.

WEEK 3 This is the time to invite friends; it's a social event or a party. In some situations, more than one Take 5 group will get together for these fun meetings. For example, a church with five or six groups may bring all of them together. This may be very informal, with everyone coming to a house, having refreshments, listening to music, talking, etc. Or it may be more structured with a theme and games. The goal is not to assemble a large group, but to have a good time together.

The purpose of this social event is to help kids learn to have fun in a positive environment and to help them feel comfortable inviting and bringing their uninvolved friends to something.

WEEK 4 This week's activity is quizzing, finding out what group members have learned. There are three kinds of quizzing: general Bible knowledge, general knowledge, and African-American history.

Bible quizzing is over the book that the group has been studying during the second week. General knowledge covers basic material that kids should be learning during the high school years. And African-American history covers important information about their cultural and racial heritage (most of the youth in the groups are African-Americans). Kids are given material to study a month ahead of time so that they can be prepared.

The quizzes may be among members of one Take 5 group or between groups. Some churches hold tournaments a couple of times during the year with all their groups. In preparation for the tournaments, kids quiz each other, sharpening their skills. Russ and the leaders try to work it out so that everybody is a winner, decreasing the potential divisiveness of competition.

WEEK 5 In the months with five of the same meeting days, the groups do service projects on the fifth week. Possible projects include singing in a church, helping someone who is sick at home, working at the church, and so forth. The purpose here is to teach kids to be givers and not just takers.

Designed for lay people who don't have the time to be creative and yet want to reach young people for Christ, the meeting cycle repeats every month. The format is very easy for volunteers to follow and use.

Besides the assignment of studying the material for quizzing, group members are expected to call each other during the week. Russ says, "This isn't anything heavy, but just merely to give a word of encouragement, share a verse, or tell the other person that they're praying for him or her. We try to establish a kind of prayer chain that the kids do themselves, and we want them to be committed to praying for one another each day. This is part of the bonding that we hope to accomplish."

"We try to establish a kind of prayer chain that the kids do themselves, and we want them to be committed to praying for one another each day. This is part of the bonding that we hope to accomplish."

Also as a part of this group building process, leaders often allow kids to solve each others' problems. This might mean putting a good algebra student with someone who is struggling in that subject. Or it might mean steering a kid with a particular problem to someone who has worked through that problem. This builds community and demonstrates the necessity of caring for each other.

Russ and his associates write the Bible studies and other curriculum. These may be brand new or may be existing materials adapted to the urban scene.

They also write their own training materials. In fact, they have just completed a manual to help recruit and train leaders. The Take 5 concept is spread through workshops and seminars. Russ says, "I think of us as trying to help small churches. We try to give away a lot of what we've learned and help them become successful, so that the local church can be successful."

The leaders don't have to use the materials that are provided. Often, Russ helps them write their own.

AT A GLANCE
Small Groups for Building Community
in Chicago, Illinois

Purpose: to build community, demonstrating what the Church should be and could be

Types of kids: any interested high school student

Leaders: adult Christians, usually married couples

Size: 5 kids and 2 "coaches" (adult couple) per group

Number of meetings each week: one

Length of each meeting: varies according to the type of meeting; Bible studies, rap times, and quizzes last about an hour

Unique features: Take 5 as a restructuring of the youth ministry for a church; the variety of activities from week to week

Materials: Russ and his associates have written their own

For more information on the Take 5 Plan, contact:

Russ Knight
President
Chicago Urban Reconciliation Enterprise
8430 S. Escanaba
Chicago, IL 60617
(312) 374-4330

TWELVE
TRAINING TO TELL
Small Groups for Evangelism Training in Mountain Lake, Minnesota

J ust saying "Mountain Lake" evokes an idyllic scene: a small, quaint town . . . serene, calm, beautiful . . . a cabin, gently swaying pines, Northern Pike and Walleye, soft waves gently lapping at the shore . . . away from the pressures and problems of everyday life.

In some sense that picture may be accurate. Certainly the town is small, and the brochures from the Office of Tourism will assure us of most of the rest. But in Mountain Lake, Minnesota, kids are just as lost as anywhere else. They struggle with peer pressure, conformity, substance abuse, identity confusion and other teenage ills. And like most kids, everywhere, they know very little about God's message, His plan, and His Son. They need direction, purpose, guidance. They need Christ.

Byron Emmert has spent most of his life in this setting. He knows the area; he knows young people; and he knows what it takes to reach them. Having ministered through both Campus Life and local churches, Byron is convinced of the effectiveness of friendship evangelism—building relationships with kids, winning the right to be heard, and then telling them about Christ.

133

Byron also believes that some of the most effective evangelists can be young people themselves, kids sharing Christ with their friends. So his ministry has consistently focused on training them to do just that. One of Byron's formats is small groups.

THE NEED

Byron decided to minister through small groups for three main reasons. First, there was his own experience. Byron had been helped through small groups as a teenager, as a college student, and as an adult. Looking back, he realized that the best training experiences he ever had were in the small group context.

Second, in reading the Gospels, Byron noticed that Jesus used a small group approach in dealing with His disciples. Beyond the large crowds, He spent many, many hours with just a few. Jesus provides a model.

Third, when Byron experimented with small groups in the first few years of his ministry, he had great results. Byron has continued with this approach because he knows it works.

Although Byron has used small groups for a variety of purposes over the years, his current emphasis is evangelism, using small groups to teach kids how to win their friends for Christ. He gives five reasons for the importance of this kind of training.

1. God calls all Christians to multiply and to build the Kingdom (see Matthew 28:18-20). One of the most obvious ways to do this is to get Christian students involved in evangelism—motivating, training, and mobilizing them to work with us (i.e., youth workers).

2. We need more people in order to get the job done. In Luke 10 we read about Jesus sending out people in pairs. As they were about to leave, Jesus said to them, "The harvest is plentiful, but the workers are few. Ask the Lord of the harvest, therefore, to send out workers into His harvest field" (verse 2).

3. We have been commanded to train others. The support for this comes from 2 Timothy 2:2 where Paul told Timothy

to entrust to others what he had been taught, so that they "will be qualified to teach others."

4. We know that young people can affect other people. Paul told Timothy not to let anyone put him down because of his age (1 Timothy 4:12), but a lot of times we do just that to our young people by overlooking them and not recognizing the significant impact they can make in evangelism. Byron says, "Over the 15 years that I've been involved in youth work, I have seen the best evangelism and the most evangelism occur when kids who are serious about their faith reach out to their non-Christian friends. They can do the job."

> "Over the 15 years that I've been involved in youth work, I have seen the best evangelism and the most evangelism occur when kids who are serious about their faith reach out to their non-Christian friends. They can do the job."

5. We know that evangelism helps a person grow spiritually. As kids take the Great Commission seriously, as they stretch their faith, and as they articulate what they believe, they mature and grow in their relationship with God. So if youth leaders want Christian kids to grow, they should get them involved in telling others about Christ.

In addition to his own ministry, Byron spends much of his time training church leaders and others in this ministry model. He has written a video series, "I've Gotta Tell You Something" (available through Youth for Christ/USA and Gospel Films) designed to be used with small groups.

THE PROCESS

Leaders
The type of leaders needed for this approach depends a great deal on the materials used and the context for its use. If, for

example, the leader is expected to teach "from scratch" (develop his or her own materials, etc.), then he or she would have to have knowledge and experience in evangelism and in teaching. In contrast, "I've Gotta Tell You Something" is volunteer-friendly, designed to be used by almost any adult who has an interest in helping kids learn how to share their faith.

> "The most effective way you can lead a small group to get involved in evangelism is to make sure you're involved in evangelism yourself. Then all of your illustrations, comments, questions, and so forth will come from the trenches, from someone who knows what he or she is talking about because you're doing it."

Even with the best materials, the small group leader must have a real heart for evangelism and should be involved in sharing Christ with his or her own peers. Byron states: "The most effective way you can lead a small group to get involved in evangelism is to make sure you're involved in evangelism yourself. Then all of your illustrations, comments, questions, and so forth will come from the trenches, from someone who knows what he or she is talking about because you're doing it."

Byron also believes that leaders will be most effective as discussion guides rather than "teachers," drawing kids into the group and helping them discover Bible truths and application for themselves.

In addition to covering certain material in the small group meetings, the leader should help relationships develop within the group. This will happen through discussing the issues, telling each other their needs, praying together, and talking about friends with whom they will be sharing the gospel. Much of this bonding will happen naturally, but the leader must set the climate.

Participants

Byron suggests organizing these groups three ways. First, there's selection. This is where Byron challenges certain individuals to join the group, to learn how to reach their friends for Christ. These kids may have demonstrated leadership ability or have expressed concern for their friends. Or they may have been growing in their faith. In any case, they are selected and challenged to get involved in personal evangelism.

The second approach involves a group that has already been organized and is meeting regularly. It could be a Sunday School class or a discipleship group. In this situation, Byron talks to the group about moving in a direction together, almost as if they were having a seminar.

Occasionally Byron has put a group together by asking for volunteers. After explaining the purpose of the group, he has those who are interested sign up.

Byron explains that the ideal participants in these small groups are FAT kids. He's not talking about their girth but about their attitude. "Fat" kids are: Faithful ... to Christ, and they can be counted on; they will follow through; Available ... to be used by God, and they can make time in their schedules for the meetings; Teachable ... open to God's direction, and they come with a desire to learn.

Group members are expected to attend every meeting and to fulfill all the assignments in between. The lessons build on each other, starting with learning the basics of the Gospel message and moving into learning how to share that message with friends, so it's important to be there every time.

Meetings

The structure of the meetings depends, to a great extent, on the personalities of the kids in the group. Byron says, "I'll do whatever is necessary to make sure that they're excited, that they're having fun, and that I'm really creating a hot environment for learning." In general, however, his format falls into the following categories: starter, discussion, lesson, application, prayer, assignment.

The groups meet once a week for about an hour to an hour

and a half. Byron believes that they need about eight weeks to cover the material thoroughly. This allows time for practical assignments and for checking on how everyone did with the applications.

Besides the weekly meetings, Byron divides the group into "prayer triplets" (groups of three). The prayer triplets get together between meetings to pray with and for each other.

Because the purpose of these small groups is so focused, the size can range from 3 to 15, plus the leader. Of course the larger groups may offer some challenges in group dynamics.

Content

No matter what material is used, there are some basics that should be covered in any attempt to train young people in evangelism. Byron organizes these basics around an acrostic, the word EVANGELISM.

E A teenager needs to ESTABLISH himself or herself in a body of believers (see Hebrews 10:24-25). Too often Christians think they can go it alone, in the Christian life and in their outreach efforts. Byron says, "Any time kids are going to get involved in evangelism, they should be prepared for spiritual warfare. That's when they need to be surrounded by other believers, by the Church. They need to be established in a local church."

V A Christian young person needs VISION for how God wants to use him or her. In 2 Corinthians 5:19-20, Paul explains that we are "ambassadors"; that is, we have been given the opportunity to be messengers of reconciliation. Kids need to see that they have a very special role to play in God's Kingdom — God wants to use them to reach others.

A A Christian needs an ATTITUDE of service. Jesus said, "For even the Son of Man did not come to be served but to serve, and to give his life as a ransom for many" (Mark 10:45). Kids should understand that if we're really going to reach the world, we must follow Christ's example and be willing to serve others.

"Any time kids are going to get involved in evangelism, they should be prepared for spiritual warfare. That's when they need to be surrounded by other believers, by the Church. They need to be established in a local church."

N Kids need to be NATURAL in the way they communicate the Good News. First Peter 3:15-16 says that we are to be ready to give an answer, "with gentleness and respect." Often kids get psyched out about "witnessing" because they have the wrong mental picture—they think they have to be super communicators with all the right answers. In reality, their main responsibility is to be ready. Sharing the faith should flow naturally in our communication with people.

G Students need to learn the importance of GOING to non-Christians. The Great Commission tells us to GO into all the world (Matthew 28:19). Byron says, "I think that the reason a lot of church kids don't share their faith is because they believe that somehow non-Christians will just sort of fall in their way. Instead of waiting for that to happen, they need to develop a strategy and a plan for going where the action is, where their non-Christian friends are."

E A young person needs to be a good EXAMPLE for Christ. Sometimes it's easy to say the right words and even to have the right answers, but then live the opposite of the message just preached. Kids need to know that a vital part of sharing the Gospel is living for Christ, in everything they do and say (Colossians 3:17).

L They need to LISTEN to non-Christians. Very often evangelistic presentations are more like canned speeches, where the presenter gives his or her spiel and then asks for a response. Byron explains, "Christ's representatives are not salespeople trying to get names on dotted lines. Instead they should care about individuals, listening carefully to where they're coming from, hearing their hurts. We have to teach kids how to listen to non-Christians."

I Christians should know how to INITIATE conversations about Christ. On the one hand, some kids are so aggressive that they scare their non-Christian friends away and turn them off to the Gospel. On the other hand, however, others are afraid to say anything to anybody about their faith and just want to be good examples. We need to teach kids both: how to be good examples and good listeners, and how to start conversations with non-Christians about spiritual issues.

S Kids must rely on the SPIRIT in their evangelism. According to Acts 1:8, effective witnessing is a by-product of the Holy Spirit working in a person's life. God works in the life of a Christian, preparing and leading him or her and even providing the words to say. God also works in the life of the non-Christian, preparing him or her to receive the message. We must help kids understand the Holy Spirit's role in evangelism, teaching them how to be sensitive to His leading and confident in His power.

M Christian young people must know the MESSAGE. This is the content of the Gospel. Byron explains: "When I have taken kids through a training course on evangelism, often I've noticed that it's easy for them to get sidetracked. They'll end up talking about religion, philosophy, or a fine point of theology. Instead, they should keep the focus on Jesus Christ, what He has done, and how we can get to know Him."

Regardless of the materials used, the EVANGELISM acrostic summarizes the basics of what Byron feels should be presented in teaching kids how to share their faith. As mentioned earlier, Byron writes his own materials (e.g., "I've Gotta Tell You Something"), but he has also used many other curricula. "I tend to let them stimulate my own thinking. Often what I read will trigger a new way that I would like to present the material. It's also a good reminder, a checklist to make sure I'm not missing something." Byron encourages youth leaders to continually research, read, and use other resources. "We must give our best to these kids. No ministry is more important than reaching our kids."

AT A GLANCE
Small Groups for Evangelism Training
in Mountain Lake, Minnesota

Purpose: to teach young people how to share their faith
with their friends

Types of kids: Faithful, Available, and Teachable Christian kids

Leaders: any Christian adult who has a heart for evangelism and wants to see young people effectively share the Gospel

Size: 3–15, plus the leader

Number of meetings each week: one small group meeting and at least one Prayer Triplet meeting

Length of each meeting: 60-90 minutes

Unique features: these small groups are focused on evangelism

Materials: "I've Gotta Tell You Something" video series

For more information on small groups for evangelism training, contact:

Byron Emmert
National Church Representative
    for Youth for Christ/USA
Box 132
Mountain Lake, MN 56159
(507) 427-3318

THIRTEEN
DEVELOPING SKILLS
Small Groups for Leadership Training in Deerfield, Illinois

T o many, college is where you prepare for the future. Boring classes, impossible assignments, all-night studying sessions, and endless exams jam the academic schedule.

Others, however, see college from the opposite perspective. Freedom, sports, girls/guys, and parties crowd out anything remotely serious.

Of course the truth lies somewhere between those two extremes. College life can be fun, and freedom is exhilarating, but there really are classes to attend and tests to pass.

Rick Dunn is a college professor. Knowing that and hearing his title of Department Chairman, you might relegate him to the first image of higher education—the musty and dusty one. If you met Rick, however, you might mistake him for a fun-loving student, and see him from the second point of view.

Again, however, the truth is in the middle. Rick is serious—and fun; theoretical—and practical. And that's a great combination for someone who trains youth ministers.

Rick came to Trinity College (Deerfield, Illinois) a few years ago after several successful years of working with kids

143

in local churches. His task was to get the youth ministry track on track, to get it going and growing. Was he successful? Consider this: youth ministry is now one of the biggest majors on campus, with 80 majors and 35 minors out of a total of 750 students.

In addition to his responsibilities at Trinity, Rick and his wife, Teresa, head Family and Adolescent Resource Ministries, and he is a writer and speaker. Rick's latest work is a series of small group Bible studies published by Victor Books.

THE NEED

Rick firmly believes that long term change and development in an individual occurs within the context of relationships. This belief has led him to minister through small groups. It's not that Rick thinks there is no place for large meetings and events. They're great for providing excitement, enthusiasm, motivation, and a sense of belonging. "But for a young person to make steps toward positive change, he or she needs feedback about his or her decisions, affirmation, correction, etc. Growth only takes place within the context of a smaller relational environment. The large group just doesn't provide that. So I'm a strong believer in small groups; that's what it takes to establish nurturing, discipling relationships."

"For a young person to make steps toward positive change, he or she needs feedback about his or her decisions, affirmation, correction, etc. Growth only takes place within the context of a smaller relational environment."

Rick also believes in small groups because of the need for meaningful relationships in our increasingly impersonal, high tech society. Kids need a place where people are actually connecting and interacting with each other.

Finally, Rick believes in this ministry approach because it gives kids the chance to develop their communication skills. Instead of being observers (as they are in so many situations), in small groups they can become active participants.

In addition to using small groups in his personal ministry, Rick uses them in his classes at Trinity. Small groups are a vital part of the curriculum.

THE PROCESS

Leaders

Rick feels strongly that small group leaders should be trained. He says, "People are often thrown into the middle of small groups, given five questions, and told to lead. They've never had the opportunity to learn and to think about what their role is and how to do it. So they are very intimidated."

That's what motivated Rick and his associates at Trinity to train their students in how to lead small groups. Their format was designed by Jana Sundene, a teacher in the youth ministry department.

In this program, upperclassmen lead discipleship small groups for underclassmen within the department. While providing ministry for the younger students, the groups also provide training for the older ones. During this time, group leaders meet regularly with Jana or Rick to evaluate the experience. Rick says, "Our upperclassmen will participate in a small group discussion, evaluation, feedback, and structured environment as they're leading the other small groups. So in a sense they are being ministered to as they are ministering to others."

Rick and Jana lead other small groups, making sure that all the youth ministry students are involved. In fact, before students lead their own groups, they will have been involved in three other small groups, one led by an upperclassman and two led by Rick or Jana. That means they will have been involved in small groups for four of their eight semesters at Trinity.

The first time students lead small groups, the structure

and materials are given to them. They are told what to do so they can concentrate on being facilitators, getting members involved, and getting the groups going. Then, after a few months, they move into the next phase where they design their format and write their curricula. All the group leaders work on this together. In the final phase, they are on their own, developing and implementing their own materials.

Rick also trains small group leaders in his own personal ministry by having students watch him in action. They participate in small groups with him, with one or two involved in each small group. After the meetings, they discuss what was done, why it was done, and where the group is heading. Together they will work on goals and shape the ministry to reach those goals.

Needless to say, Rick and Jana's students are well-prepared to develop an effective small group ministry with high school students. Many of them are involved with kids at area churches and parachurch ministries.

Rick emphasizes that it is important for small group leaders to see themselves first as ministers, and second as leaders. In other words, they should be investing themselves in the lives of the kids during the week, not just at the meetings. This means checking in with each group member at least once a week, to do something together, to talk things over, or to just see how the person is doing.

Rick believes that leading small groups is a skill that must be learned and developed. It's not natural. Rick states: "We tend to think that there are some people who are just naturally gifted at leading a group. But I've never seen anyone who didn't have to practice, and work at it, and learn what it means to be a small group leader. And the number one skill that has to be learned is how to listen. If you can learn to be a listener, you can be a small group leader."

Participants

In the youth ministry track at Trinity College, all the participants of the small groups are college students. And they have to get involved as part of their education. Obviously they come to the groups highly motivated. This doesn't mean that they are all alike or that there are no problems. Every group has its unique personalities, adjustments, and group dynamics. But these young men and women are operating on a different level than the typical high school group.

Rick recommends the following principles when putting small groups together, especially with high school students. When groups are organized this way, kids will be more likely to get involved.

1. **Have a specific purpose.** In other words, don't just say to kids, "We're going to do small groups." That's not motivational. Instead, explain why you're putting the groups together and what you hope to accomplish.

2. **Build on success.** This means beginning with young people who are motivated to participate and giving them a good experience. Rick adds: "Have one or two small groups and do those really well, so that the students who participate will come out talking about what a great experience they had. Then, the next time, divide those two groups into six groups, encouraging each set of kids to bring a couple of friends, and so on."

3. **Explain how the groups fit into the total program.** In other words, the students you hope to reach should know that you're not doing this new program in isolation or as an afterthought.

4. **Fold the small groups into the existing ministry structure.** Don't add another night of the week; kids are busy enough with homework, sports, and other actitivities. Instead, break into groups in place of another program element, or at least have the groups meet on the same night and place that your kids already meet.

5. **Organize groups of kids with something in common.** A 13-year-old boy in the same group as a 17-year-old girl can mean trouble. Watch out for too many different types of people in a group. And remember that kids like to be with someone they know.

According to Rick, the ideal participant in small groups is motivated and already has a good relationship with the leader. This will make the meetings run smoothly and help the group grow together.

Meetings

Rick emphasizes that the three vital ingredients for any small group are vulnerability, accountability, and responsibility. Vulnerability means being open and honest. In the meetings, all the participants (kids and leader) should feel free to express their real feelings, learning more and more about themselves.

Accountability means that group members make the effort to learn and grow together. The group is not just for fellowship and food; it's for moving forward in the Christian life. And that will take work.

Responsibility means that members are committed to the group, being at the meetings, etc., and committed to the others in the group, praying for them, supporting them. It means helping the others make progress in their spiritual journeys.

Rick plans for his small groups to be together for about 60–90 minutes, with the meeting itself taking 45 of them. Kids always need time to greet each other and to socialize before they get down to business. In this regard, it's important for the leader to be flexible, not afraid to run a little longer, stop a little sooner, go off on a tangent, or take a detour when necessary. The leader shouldn't feel that he or she has to get through the material if the group's needs warrant going in another direction.

Concerning group size, Rick thinks six is ideal, with no more than eight. Normally the group should meet for 6–8 weeks and then evaluate and reorganize, but that would depend on the purpose and the make-up of the small group. Rick gives this example: "If you're working with 25 kids in a youth group and you want to do four small groups, it's a good idea to do six weeks on, take a week or two off, and then restructure the groups a bit."

Content

The content covered in the small groups depends on the purpose of the group. Rick says, "Sometimes I've led Bible study small groups where we've studied a book in the Bible or we've looked at a topic, like love or grace, in the New

> "If you're working with 25 kids in a youth group and you want to do 4 small groups, it's a good idea to do 6 weeks on, take a week or two off, and then restructure the groups a bit."

Testament. At other times, the agenda has been to take something that is happening in the group, a problem to solve, a need to meet, or a concern to address and go that direction."

Whatever content you choose, the key is to have a specific goal so that at the end you can say, "Here are the truths we've learned; here are the things we've shared; here's the progress we've made."

Materials

As we've already seen, Rick and his associates write the materials used by his college students. Group leaders at Trinity College use those materials until they learn to develop their own.

With high school students, Rick has used resources from Group Publishing, Victor Books, and a number of other sources. As mentioned earlier, Rick has written a series of small group studies for Victor Books. Called "SonPower Small Group Studies," these studies focus on various topics (e.g., Getting to Know God, Understanding Feelings, and Sex and Dating). Each study has student books and a leader's guide.

Rick believes that it is important to keep checking out the available resources. He states: "One of the dangers in leading a small group is that no matter who we are or how much we've studied, we tend to get into ruts. So one of the things I'm challenged to do is to try to make most of the six weeks different. To do that, I have to keep looking for different methods and different styles to keep from always doing the same thing the same way. I want the meetings to be fresh, filled with anticipation and excitement."

AT A GLANCE
Small Groups for Leadership Development
in Deerfield, Illinois

Purpose: to train college students and others to lead their own small groups

Types of kids: college students in the Youth Ministry courses at Trinity College

Leaders: upperclassmen college students, Rick, and Jana Sundene

Size: 6–8, including the leader

Number of meetings each week: one

Length of each meeting: 60-90 minutes, with 45 of those for discussion/teaching time

Unique features: students are trained to lead groups by being a part of a group

Materials: Rick and his associates have written the materials for the leaders to use as they begin their groups

For more information on leadership development groups, contact:

Youth Ministry Dept.
Trinity College
2077 Half Day Road
Deerfield, IL 60187
(708) 317-7147

FOURTEEN
THE RIGHT MOVES
Choosing the Small Group Approach to Fit Your Ministry Needs

N ow it's up to you. You've read what it takes to build an effective small group ministry. You've learned the "why's," the "what's" (who should be there and what happens when they get there), and the "hows" (how to organize a group, how to lead a group, how to lead a discussion). And you've seen eight successful small group ministries up close and personal.

Now that you know it all, what are you going to do? How will you put what you've learned into practice?

Whatever you do, please don't simply copy one of the profiles, forcing your kids into a mold that I've described in chapters 6–13. The profiles are illustrations of the ministry principles applied in real life, not formulae to follow. Remember, your kids are special; your ministry is unique.

Instead, take the appropriate pieces from a number of the profiled ministries and construct a ministry that fits your kids, your gifts, and your calling.

To facilitate this process, I've included a set of questions that should help you analyze your situation and put together the right small group approach.

It's your move.

PURPOSE—the ultimate goal(s) of your ministry with young people

1. What do you hope to accomplish in the lives of your kids? What are your goals?

2. Which of these goals might be more effectively reached through small groups? Why?

3. Which small group(s) (profiled in chapters 6–13) has (have) goals that are most like the one(s) you listed in Question 2?

PHILOSOPHY

1. What ministry "bottom lines" must be present in all of your youth ministry programs?

2. Which of the profiled small groups seem consistent with your philosophy of ministry?

3. What adaptations do you think you might have to make in any of the small group approaches so that they reflect your philosophy?

4. How would small groups fit into the rest of your ministry program?

PLAN

Participants
1. Considering your ministry goals, what kids would you like to see involved in small groups?

2. How would these young people be "recruited"?

3. Why would they want to join a small group?

4. Who will determine what kids are in which small groups?

5. What criteria will be used to make that determination?

6. How many kids would be in each small group?

7. What would the small group participants do after their initial small group experience (i.e., would they stay in the same group, join another group, lead a group, do something else)?

Meetings

1. When would the small groups meet?

2. How long would each meeting be?

3. How would each meeting be divided or organized?

4. How many times would each small group meet before they took a break? What would happen then?

Content

1. How would you decide what the small groups should cover in their meetings?

2. What would be the leader's role in choosing the meeting content?

3. What content would you like to see covered during the first six weeks of small group meetings?

4. What would come next?

5. What materials would the small groups use?

6. Where would you get those materials?

Leaders
1. Who would lead the small groups? What kind of people do you want?

2. If you don't already have a group of potential leaders, where will you find them and how will you recruit them?

3. What kind of training would you require for your small group leaders?

4. When and how long would you train them and what would the training cover?

5. What would you require your leaders to do (i.e., before meetings, during meetings, between meetings)? How can you minimize their time commitments?

BONUS QUESTION: How many more copies of this book will you buy? (Note: I recommend one per small group leader.)

THE RIGHT STUFF

This is not an exhaustive bibliography of resources for small group ministry. It is a collection of books, journals, and other materials that I have found helpful. Check out your Christian bookstore for more. Most Christian publishers of youth ministry materials (e.g., Scripture Press/Victor Books, David C. Cook, Zondervan/Youth Specialists, Harvest House, Gospel Light, Standard Publishing, Group Publishing) have curricula that can be adapted for small group use.

In addition to the resources listed, most of the leaders of the small group ministries profiled in chapters 6–13 have written their own materials. Contact them directly for more information.

RESOURCES FOR SMALL GROUP MINISTRY WITH YOUTH

General Youth Ministry Books and Journals

Benson, Warren S. and Mark H. Senter III, eds. *The Complete Book of Youth Ministry*. Chicago, Ill.: Moody Press, 1989. With 33 articles written by a variety of youth experts, this volume covers all aspects of youth ministry.

Burns, Jim. *The Youth Builder*. Eugene, Ore.: Harvest House Publishers 1988
This is an excellent resource for planning, organizing, and implementing a church youth ministry. Written by a youth ministry veteran, the book covers everything from understanding relational youth ministry and building relationships to planning programs.

Collins, Gary R. *Christian Counseling: A Comprehensive Guide*. Waco, Tx.: Word Books, 1980.
As the title suggests, this book is packed with helpful counsel for just about every occasion—a valuable resource.

Dausey, Gary, ed. *The Youth Leader's Sourcebook*. Grand Rap-

ids, Mich.: Zondervan Publishing House, 1983.
Drawing on the collective wisdom of a number of youth experts, this volume provides a complete view of youth ministry, with practical ideas for building a foundation, developing an environment, planning activities, and sharpening skills.

Kesler, Jay and Ron Beers, eds. *Parents and Teenagers.* Wheaton, Ill.; Victor Books, 1984.
This 700-page reference work contains hundreds of articles on almost every conceivable topic relating to parents and teens. It's a practical resource for parents and youth workers.

Olson, Keith. *Counseling Teenagers.* Loveland, Colo.: Group Books, 1984. This is an exhaustive reference work for counseling, covering a multitude of problems and situations.

Rowley, William J. *Equipped to Care: A Youth Worker's Guide to Counseling Teenagers,* Wheaton, Ill.: Victor Books, 1990.
This is a non-intimidating how-to handbook on counseling teenagers, written especially for the lay youth worker.

Spotts, Dwight and David Veerman. *Reaching Out to Troubled Youth.* Wheaton, Ill.: Victor Books, 1987.
This book is for Christian adults who care about troubled young people and want to reach them for Christ. See especially the chapters on communicating the Gospel and on teaching the Bible.

Strommen, Merton P. and A. Irene. *Five Cries of Parents.* San Francisco, Calif.: Harper and Row, 1985.
Written as a result of an extensive study of early adolescents and their parents by the Search Institute, this book provides a wealth of in-depth information for both youth workers and parents.

Veerman, David. *Reaching Kids before High School.* Wheaton,

Ill.: Victor Books, 1990.
Written to help motivate and mobilize professional and volunteer youth workers, this book lays a foundation for ministry based on the needs and characteristics of early adolescents and then outlines practical strategies for building an effective ministry.

Veerman, David. *Youth Evangelism: When They're in the Neighborhood, but Not in the Fold.* Wheaton, Ill.: Victor Books, 1988.
This book is about reaching kids for Christ, and it is written for Christian adults, not just professional youth workers. After describing and analyzing youth culture, it explains how to make contact with kids, build relationships, and share the Gospel. There is a chapter on leading small groups.

Youth Worker Journal. El Cajon, Calif.: Youth Specialties.
Written for professional youth workers, this quarterly journal is packed with practical articles covering all aspects of youth ministry.

Small Group Ministry Books
Griffin, Em. *Getting Together: A Guide for Good Groups.* Downers Grove, Ill.: InterVarsity Press, 1982.
A professor and veteran youth worker, Dr. Griffin has led hundreds of small groups. From his knowledge and experience, he shares insights and instructions for organizing and running effective small groups.

Nicholas, Ron, coordinating editor. *Good Things Come in Small Groups.*
Downers Grove, Ill.: InterVarsity Press, 1985.
Written by members of small group, this book gives an insider's view of they dynamics of good gorup life. Although written primarily for groups of Christian adults, there is much practical help, especially in the section entitled "Basics of Small Groups."

Plueddeman, Jim and Carol. *Pilgrims in Progress: Growing through Groups.*
Wheaton, Ill.: Harold Shaw Publishers, 1990.
This is a well-written book on the value of small groups for the Church. The chapters on aims and methods are especially helpful.

Small Group Bible Studies
Life Application Bible Studies. Wheaton, Ill.: Tyndale House Publishers.
These award-winning Bible studies help group members get into the Word and apply it to their lives. Each booklet contains the entire text of Scripture with all the notes from the *Life Application Bible* and 13 Bible study lessons (in the back). The studies currently cover all the New Testament and much of the Old. Most are available in the New International Version, and some in The Living Bible. Especially good for use with high schoolers are Genesis, Daniel, Mark, John, and James.

Life Application Bible for Students. Wheaton, Ill.: Tyndale House Publishers, 1992.
Hot off the press, this is the only Bible with the notes and helps written by youth experts for young people. At the end of each Bible book, there is a section entitled "Megathemes" which highlights the major themes of the book and gives a number of questions for discussing each theme in a group.

Serendipity Study Bible for Groups. Lyman Coleman, editor. Grand Rapids, Mich.: Zondervan Publishing Company, 1988.
Designed especially for groups, this Bible is divided into study sections with helpful insights, openers, and questions for each section.

Serendipity Youth Bible Study Series, by Lyman Coleman and Denny Rydberg. Serendipity, 1989.
These are issue-oriented studies for young people covering morality, identity, lifestyle, friendship, and other important topics. Each study has seven lessons.

Other Small Group Resources

Discipleship Journal. Colorado Springs, Colo.: The Navigators. Published monthly, this outstanding magazine serves the Navigator ministry and anyone else helping others develop a deeper relationship with Christ. Each issue contains a special section for small groups. Although written primarily with adults in mind, there are many helpful ideas for all types of small groups.

SonPower Small Group Studies, by Richard Dunn, Wheaton, Ill.: Victor, 1990.
Each book contains six sessions and is available in both student and leader's formats.

- *Can We Talk, God?* — building a close relationship with God
- *Can't Fight the Feelings* — understanding and handling our emotions
- *Why Not Love All of Me?* — accepting ourselves and relating to others
- *Where Do You Think Sex Came From:* — dealing with sexuality and sensuality

The following materials are published by Youth for Christ/USA. See your local YFC chapter or contact YFC Sales for more information:
P.O. Box 228822
Denver, CO 80222
(303) 843-9000

First S.T.E.P.S in the Christian Life — a fourteen-day guide for immediate follow-up for new Christains. Written by Neil Wilson, it is available in individual booklets (8 ½" x 11") or a photocopy master.

Guaranteed in Writing — a follow-up book for new Christians. Good for use in small groups, this is also published by Navigators as "Lessons on Assurance."

I Gotta Tell You Something — A video series for training young people in personal evangelism. Designed and written by Byron Emmert, the seven sessions come on two tapes. A leader's guide is also available.

Honest to God — the curriculum for evangelistic small groups. Written by Dave Bartlett, this is the material described in chapter 8 of this book.

Campus Life Guide to Student Leadership — a study guide for developing students into leaders in your group. It teaches how to be a leader and the responsibilities of Christian leadership.

LUG Manuals 1 & 2 — resources for small group study. They include topical studies, Bible book studies, and a series on the Chronicles of Narnia.

Breaking Free — a study guide to help teach "how to get going and keep growing as a Christ." Written for those with lower reading skills, this is an excellent resource for junior high ministry.

Stop, Look, Listen, Go — a guide on learning how to make decisions. The second in the life skills series, this is also great for junior highers.

How to Get What You Need — lessons on how to communicate, with other people and with God. The third in the life skills series. Use with kids who are slow readers and with junior highers.